sports Outreach

Topical Bible

THE ATHLETE'S TOPICAL BIBLE

Gordon Thiessen, The Athlete's Topical Bible

ISBN 1-887002-06-5

Cross Training Publishing
317 West Second Street
Grand Island, NE 68801
(800) 430-8588

This book is manufactured in the United States of America.

Library of Congress Cataloging in Publication Data in Progress.

Published by Cross Training Publishing
317 West Second Street
Grand Island, NE 68801
1-800-430-8588
Publisher website: www.crosstrainingpublishing.com

Foreword by Steve Connor

Have you ever picked up the Bible and wondered, 'where should I start'? Have you ever asked yourself, 'Does God really care about my sport'? Have you ever wanted to dig deep into spiritual truths only to be somehow discouraged? If you have, don't worry you are not alone! The Sports Outreach Scotland Topical Bible can be a good place to start.

This is a great tool for young Christians trying to Find their way through the seemingly endless complexities of Scripture. It is also beneficial for the mature Christian as a quick reference for valuable specific subjects & unique pressures that pertain to a sports person. It Is an endless challenge to reconcile one's personal Christian faith with his or her daily life. Perhaps, it is even harder to live the Christian life in the sporting arena. You will be surprised at how much God has to say about your participation in sport. The Bible says in Colossians 3:23, "Whatever you do, work at it with all your heart, as working for the Lord, not men." "Whatever" includes how we live our lives and play our sports.

I certainly do not advise The Sports Outreach Topical Bible to be the only Bible the Christian sports person needs; rather it is a valuable tool that will enhance one's love for God's Word. I suggest you find a topic in this book that interests you, then go back to your Bible and read the whole paragraph, better yet try to read the whole chapter.

Thanks 'Big-Time' to Gordon Thiessen and Cross Training Publishing for your insight in compiling this book and your generosity to reformat it for a Scottish audience.

A special thank-you to the Scottish Bible Society, for your commitment and desire, to bring the Word of God to the World of Sport!

Steve Connor
Director
Sports Outreach Scotland
PO Box 5349 Crieff
Perthshire
PH6 2LJ
www.sportsoutreach.com

ON YOUR MARKS

Paul explains that the Christian life is like running a race (1 Corinthians 24-25). Competitive sportsmen and women have to go through a strict training programme. It requires hard work, determination, discipline, (not to mention early mornings and a 'go for it' attitude).

Sometimes the Christian life can be really hard work and requires us to be determined; it's not all running on flat ground. There are a few steep hills to climb and hurdles to jump over until we 'win the prize'. Let's really go for it and be ACTIVE for God. Read Hebrews 12:1-2.

TWO TOUGH QUESTIONS
that we all have to answer:

Do you know for certain that if you died tonight you would go to Heaven?

If you were standing before Jesus at Heaven's gates and He asked, "Why should you come in?", what would you say?

Here's how you can know for sure! It's all in the Bible!

1.   You are loved. God loves you and has a purpose & plan for your life. Jesus Himself said, "I came that you may have life, and have it to the full." That means you!

2.   Sin is real. Even though God loves you and me, we don't always choose the good things HE gives us. We want to do it our own way - not His. The Bible says, "Yes, all have sinned and fall short of God's glorious idea for us" and "Sin's payment for us is death" (separation from God).

3.   God has the answer. God doesn't want you to die. That's why He came to earth in the person of Jesus Christ, to die for YOU on the cross, so you could have eternal life. Scripture says: "For God so loved the world that He gave his only Son, that whoever believes in Him shall not perish but have eternal life."

4.   The choice is yours. You can know God's love—you can live life to the fullest—when you open your life to Jesus Christ and you choose to follow His way. Again Jesus says, "Look I stand at the door (of your heart) and knock, open the door."

You, too, can start this new life by following these four steps:

REALISE that God is holy and perfect. Though we are sinners and
cannot save ourselves, He loves us.
RECOGNISE who Jesus is and what He has done as our substitute.
REPENT by turning to God, away from sin and seeking forgiveness.
RECEIVE Jesus Christ by faith as Saviour and Lord by committing yourself to Him.

A HELPFUL PRAYER

Dear God,

I must admit that there have been many times in my life when I know that I have said and done things that were wrong. Please forgive me. It comes as a great relief to find out that although I can't wipe out the past, you can.

I take this opportunity to receive your forgiveness and believe that your Son Jesus Christ paid for the price of salvation, and that his death on a cross was for me, God in my place.

I don't understand how it all works, but I now put my trust in you for my future. Please help me to know you better, and give me the strength of your Spirit to help me to live differently from now on.

Thank you for listening and answering this prayer.

For additional books and resources available
from Cross Training Publishing, contact us at:

Cross Training Publishing
P.O. Box 1541
Grand Island, NE 68802
(308) 384-5762

CONTENTS *of*

ON THE FIELD

CONTENTS

_of_

OFF THE COURT

TABLE of CONTENTS

X'S AND O'S OF THE FAITH

TABLE of CONTENTS

COACHES

What is The Athlete's Topical Bible?

It's a collection of athletic oriented topics from the *New International Translation* of the Bible. Each verse is listed with its reference. *The Athlete's Topical Bible* includes four sections or quarters: First Quarter: On The Field (Athletic oriented Bible verses) Second Quarter: Off The Court (Practical Bible verses for everyday living) Third Quarter: X's & O's of the Faith (The Basics or fundamentals of the faith) Fourth Quarter: Coaches (Special section for coaches).

How should I use this Bible?

First, it can be used for personal Bible study. You can choose any topic and study or memorize the verses that go with each section.

Second, it can be used with a group. Many of the topics can easily be covered in a Bible study. It can be used as a helpful reference for whatever study your group would like to do.

Third, it can be used as an outreach tool. The goal of this Bible is to get the reader into the entire Word of God. However, some athletes will find both the look and feel of this Bible more relevant to their lives than the complete Bible. Hopefully, *The Athlete's Topical Bible* will be the first step in helping athletes to commit themselves to Christ and then to follow in His footsteps by obeying His Word.

ON THE FIELD

Quarter

1

THE ATHLETE'S TOPICAL BIBLE

Every prudent man acts out of knowledge, but a fool exposes his folly.

Proverbs 13:16

"Ask and it will be given to you; seek and you will find; knock and the door will be opened to you.

Matthew 7:7

A simple man believes anything, but a prudent man gives thought to his steps. A wise man fears the LORD and shuns evil, but a fool is hotheaded and reckless.

Proverbs 14:15,16

"Suppose one of you wants to build a tower. Will he not first sit down and estimate the cost to see if he has enough money to complete it?

For if he lays the foundation and is not able to finish it, everyone who sees it will ridicule him, saying, `This fellow began to build and was not able to finish.' "

Or suppose a king is about to go to war against another king. Will he not first sit down and consider whether he is able with ten thousand men to oppose the one coming against him with twenty thousand?

Luke 14:28-31

The prudent see danger and take refuge, but the simple keep going and suffer for it.

Proverbs 27:12

Whoever gives heed to instruction prospers, and blessed is he who trusts in the LORD.

Proverbs 16:20

The heart of the discerning acquires knowledge; the ears of the wise seek it out.

Proverbs 18:15

Make plans by seeking advice; if you wage war, obtain guidance.

Proverbs 20:18

The plans of the diligent lead to profit as surely as haste leads to poverty.

Proverbs 21:5

For waging war you need guidance, and for victory many advisers.

Proverbs 24:6

For those God foreknew he also predestined to be conformed to the likeness of his Son, that he might be the firstborn among many brothers.

Romans 8:29

"No one can serve two masters. Either he will hate the one and love the other, or he will be devoted to the one and despise the other. You cannot serve both God and Money.

Matthew 6:24

Plans fail for lack of counsel, but with many advisers they succeed.

Proverbs 15:22

Since, then, you have been raised with Christ, set your hearts on things above, where Christ is seated at the right hand of God.

Colossians 3:1

THE ATHLETE'S TOPICAL BIBLE

So we make it our goal to please him, whether we are at home in the body or away from it.

2 Corinthians 5:9

So whether you eat or drink or whatever you do, do it all for the glory of God.

1 Corinthians 10:31

Now to him who is able to do immeasurably more than all we ask or imagine, according to his power that is at work within us.

Ephesians 3:20

Be very careful, then, how you live—not as unwise but as wise, making the most of every opportunity, because the days are evil.

Ephesians 5:15-16

Brothers, I do not consider myself yet to have taken hold of it. But one thing I do: Forgetting what is behind and straining toward what is ahead, I press on toward the goal to win the prize for which God has called me heavenward in Christ Jesus.

Philippians 3:13 -14

Are you so foolish? After beginning with the Spirit, are you now trying to attain your goal by human effort?

Galatians 3:3

This is the confidence we have in approaching God: that if we ask anything according to his will, he hears us.

1 John 5:14

"`Do not seek revenge or bear a grudge against one of your people, but love your neighbor as yourself. I am the LORD.

Leviticus 19:18

For if you forgive men when they sin against you, your heavenly Father will also forgive you.

Matthew 6:14

Do not say, "I'll pay you back for this wrong!" Wait for the LORD, and he will deliver you.

Proverbs 20:22

If he sins against you seven times in a day, and seven times comes back to you and says, `I repent,' forgive him."

Luke 17:4

O LORD my God, I take refuge in you; save and deliver me from all who pursue me.

Psalm 7:1

To you, O LORD, I lift up my soul; in you I trust, O my God. Do not let me be put to shame, nor let my enemies triumph over me.

Psalm 25:1,2

And the Lord's servant must not quarrel; instead, he must be kind to everyone, able to teach, not resentful.

2 Timothy 2:24

Do not repay anyone evil for evil. Be careful to do what is right in the eyes of everybody.

Romans 12:17

THE ATHLETE'S TOPICAL BIBLE

Resentment kills a fool, and envy slays the simple.

Job 5:2

My lips will not speak wickedness, and my tongue will utter no deceit.

Job 27:4

Set a guard over my mouth, O LORD; keep watch over the door of my lips.

Psalm 141:3

"In your anger do not sin": Do not let the sun go down while you are still angry.

Ephesians 4:26

My dear brothers, take note of this: Everyone should be quick to listen, slow to speak and slow to become angry.

James 1:19

The mouth of the righteous is a fountain of life, but violence overwhelms the mouth of the wicked.

When words are many, sin is not absent, but he who holds his tongue is wise.

Proverbs 10:11,19

A fool shows his annoyance at once, but a prudent man overlooks an insult.

Proverbs 12:16

He who guards his lips guards his life, but he who speaks rashly will come to ruin.

Proverbs 13:3

A patient man has great understanding, but a quick-tempered man displays folly.

Proverbs 14:29

A gentle answer turns away wrath, but a harsh word stirs up anger.

Proverbs 15:1

Likewise the tongue is a small part of the body, but it makes great boasts. Consider what a great forest is set on fire by a small spark.

James 3:5

But I tell you that men will have to give account on the day of judgment for every careless word they have spoken.

Matthew 12:36

But now you must rid yourselves of all such things as these: anger, rage, malice, slander, and filthy language from your lips.

Colossians 3:8

Keep your tongue from evil and your lips from speaking lies.

Psalm 34:13

I said, "I will watch my ways and keep my tongue from sin; I will put a muzzle on my mouth as long as the wicked are in my presence."

Psalm 39:1

A man who lacks judgment derides his neighbor, but a man of understanding holds his tongue.

Proverbs 11:12

7

All the believers were one in heart and mind. No one claimed that any of his possessions was his own, but they shared everything they had.

Acts 4:32

How good and pleasant it is when brothers live together in unity!

Psalm 133:1

If you have any encouragement from being united with Christ, if any comfort from his love, if any fellowship with the Spirit, if any tenderness and compassion, then make my joy complete by being like-minded, having the same love, being one in spirit and purpose.

Do nothing out of selfish ambition or vain conceit, but in humility consider others better than yourselves.

Philippians 2:1-3

Hold them in the highest regard in love because of their work. Live in peace with each other.

1 Thessalonians 5:13

Finally, all of you, live in harmony with one another; be sympathetic, love as brothers, be compassionate and humble.

1 Peter 3:8

Do not let any unwholesome talk come out of your mouths, but only what is helpful for building others up according to their needs, that it may benefit those who listen.

Ephesians 4:29

Instead, speaking the truth in love, we will in all things grow up into him who is the Head, that is, Christ.

From him the whole body, joined and held together by every supporting ligament, grows and builds itself up in love, as each part does its work.

Ephesians 4:15,16

Just as each of us has one body with many members, and these members do not all have the same function, so in Christ we who are many form one body, and each member belongs to all the others.

We have different gifts, according to the grace given us. If a man's gift is prophesying, let him use it in proportion to his faith.

If it is serving, let him serve; if it is teaching, let him teach; if it is encouraging, let him encourage; if it is contributing to the needs of others, let him give generously; if it is leadership, let him govern diligently; if it is showing mercy, let him do it cheerfully.

Romans 12:4-8

Therefore encourage one another and build each other up, just as in fact you are doing.

1 Thessalonians 5:11

Two are better than one, because they have a good return for their work:

Ecclesiastes 4:9

If you have any encouragement from being united with Christ, if any comfort from his love, if any fellowship with the Spirit, if any tenderness and compassion.

Philippians 2:1

Refrain from anger and turn from wrath; do not fret --it leads only to evil.

Psalm 37:8

By standing firm you will gain life.

Luke 21:19

Whatever you do, work at it with all your heart, as working for the Lord, not for men.

Colossians 3:23

On the contrary, we speak as men approved by God to be entrusted with the gospel. We are not trying to please men but God, who tests our hearts.

1 Thessalonians 2:4

But whoever listens to me will live in safety and be at ease, without fear of harm."

Proverbs 1:33

Love is patient, love is kind. It does not envy, it does not boast, it is not proud.

It is not rude, it is not self-seeking, it is not easily angered, it keeps no record of wrongs.

1 Corinthians 13:4,5

Let us not become weary in doing good, for at the proper time we will reap a harvest if we do not give up.

Galatians 6:9

You need to persevere so that when you have done the will of God, you will receive what he has promised.

Hebrews 10:36

And we urge you, brothers, warn those who are idle, encourage the timid, help the weak, be patient with everyone.

1 Thessalonians 5:14

A hot-tempered man stirs up dissension, but a patient man calms a quarrel.

Proverbs 15:18

But now, this is what the LORD says-- he who created you, O Jacob, he who formed you, O Israel: "Fear not, for I have redeemed you; I have summoned you by name; you are mine.

When you pass through the waters, I will be with you; and when you pass through the rivers, they will not sweep over you. When you walk through the fire, you will not be burned; the flames will not set you ablaze.

Isaiah 43:1,2

I sought the LORD, and he answered me; he delivered me from all my fears.

Psalm 34:4

So do not fear, for I am with you; do not be dismayed, for I am your God. I will strengthen you and help you; I will uphold you with my righteous right hand.

Isaiah 41:10

For you did not receive a spirit that makes you a slave again to fear, but you received the Spirit of sonship. And by him we cry, "Abba, Father."

Romans 8:15

Be joyful in hope, patient in affliction, faithful in prayer.

Romans 12:12

THE ATHLETE'S TOPICAL BIBLE

Be strong and take heart, all you who hope in the LORD.

Psalm 31:24

"Be strong and courageous, because you will lead these people to inherit the land I swore to their forefathers to give them.

Joshua 1:6

Cast all your anxiety on him because he cares for you.

1 Peter 5:7

I can do everything through him who gives me strength.

Philippians 4:13

Wait for the LORD; be strong and take heart and wait for the LORD.

Psalm 27:14

"But now, Lord, what do I look for? My hope is in you.

Psalm 39:7

Trust in the LORD with all your heart and lean not on your own understanding; in all your ways acknowledge him, and he will make your paths straight.

Proverbs 3:5,6

David was greatly distressed because the men were talking of stoning him; each one was bitter in spirit because of his sons and daughters. But David found strength in the LORD his God.

1 Samuel 30:6

"`If you can'?" said Jesus. "Everything is possible for him who believes."

Immediately the boy's father exclaimed, "I do believe; help me overcome my unbelief!"

Mark 9:23,24

Therefore I tell you, whatever you ask for in prayer, believe that you have received it, and it will be yours.

Mark 11:24

But if we hope for what we do not yet have, we wait for it patiently.

Who shall separate us from the love of Christ? Shall trouble or hardship or persecution or famine or nakedness or danger or sword?

As it is written: "For your sake we face death all day long; we are considered as sheep to be slaughtered."

No, in all these things we are more than conquerors through him who loved us.

For I am convinced that neither death nor life, neither angels nor demons, neither the present nor the future, nor any powers, neither height nor depth, nor anything else in all creation, will be able to separate us from the love of God that is in Christ Jesus our Lord.

Romans 8:25,35,36-39

Being strengthened with all power according to his glorious might so that you may have great endurance and patience, and joyfully giving thanks to the Father, who has qualified you to share in the inheritance of the saints in the kingdom of light.

Colossians 1:11,12

Do not fret because of evil men or be envious of those who do wrong;

Psalm 37:1

Let us not become conceited, provoking and envying each other.

Galatians 5:26

And I saw that all labor and all achievement spring from man's envy of his neighbor. This too is meaningless, a chasing after the wind.

Ecclesiastes 4:4

A heart at peace gives life to the body, but envy rots the bones.

Proverbs 14:30

Love is patient, love is kind. It does not envy, it does not boast, it is not proud.

1 Corinthians 13:4

But if you harbor bitter envy and selfish ambition in your hearts, do not boast about it or deny the truth.

James 3:14

Anger is cruel and fury overwhelming, but who can stand before jealousy?

Proverbs 27:4

Therefore, rid yourselves of all malice and all deceit, hypocrisy, envy, and slander of every kind.

1 Peter 2:1

THE ATHLETE'S TOPICAL BIBLE

14

Jesus replied, "I tell you the truth, if you have faith and do not doubt, not only can you do what was done to the fig tree, but also you can say to this mountain, `Go, throw yourself into the sea,' and it will be done.

If you believe, you will receive whatever you ask for in prayer."

Matthew 21:21,22

He replied, "If you have faith as small as a mustard seed, you can say to this mulberry tree, `Be uprooted and planted in the sea,' and it will obey you.

Luke 17:6

"`If you can'?" said Jesus. "Everything is possible for him who believes."

Mark 9:23

In addition to all this, take up the shield of faith, with which you can extinguish all the flaming arrows of the evil one.

Ephesians 6:16

So do not fear, for I am with you; do not be dismayed, for I am your God. I will strengthen you and help you; I will uphold you with my righteous right hand.

Isaiah 41:10

But when he asks, he must believe and not doubt, because he who doubts is like a wave of the sea, blown and tossed by the wind.

James 1:6

THE ATHLETE'S TOPICAL BIBLE

Therefore encourage one another and build each other up, just as in fact you are doing.

1 Thessalonians 5:11

David was greatly distressed because the men were talking of stoning him; each one was bitter in spirit because of his sons and daughters. But David found strength in the LORD his God.

1 Samuel 30:6

Cast your cares on the LORD and he will sustain you; he will never let the righteous fall.

Psalm 55:22

Though I walk in the midst of trouble, you preserve my life; you stretch out your hand against the anger of my foes, with your right hand you save me.

The LORD will fulfill [his purpose] for me; your love, O LORD, endures forever-- do not abandon the works of your hands.

Psalm 138:7,8

When you pass through the waters, I will be with you; and when you pass through the rivers, they will not sweep over you. When you walk through the fire, you will not be burned; the flames will not set you ablaze.

Isaiah 43:2

If you love those who love you, what reward will you get? Are not even the tax collectors doing that?

Matthew 5:39-46

16

"In your anger do not sin" : Do not let the sun go down while you are still angry, and do not give the devil a foothold.

Ephesians 4:26,27

Love is patient, love is kind. It does not envy, it does not boast, it is not proud.

It is not rude, it is not self-seeking, it is not easily angered, it keeps no record of wrongs.

Love does not delight in evil but rejoices with the truth.

It always protects, always trusts, always hopes, always perseveres.

Love never fails. But where there are prophecies, they will cease; where there are tongues, they will be stilled; where there is knowledge, it will pass away.

1 Corinthians 13:4-8

A man's wisdom gives him patience; it is to his glory to overlook an offense.

Proverbs 19:11

Forgive us our debts, as we also have forgiven our debtors.

Matthew 6:12

And when you stand praying, if you hold anything against anyone, forgive him, so that your Father in heaven may forgive you your sins. "

Mark 11:25

Do not repay evil with evil or insult with insult, but with blessing, because to this you were called so that you may inherit a blessing.

1 Peter 3:9

THE **A**THLETE'S **T**OPICAL **B**IBLE

Finally, be strong in the Lord and in his mighty power.

Ephesians 6:10

Let us not become weary in doing good, for at the proper time we will reap a harvest if we do not give up.

Galatians 6:9

The LORD is close to the brokenhearted and saves those who are crushed in spirit.

Psalm 34:18

When I said, "My foot is slipping," your love, O LORD, supported me.

Psalm 94:18

I sought the LORD, and he answered me; he delivered me from all my fears.

Psalm 34:4

So don't be afraid; you are worth more than many sparrows.

Matthew 10:31

Cast all your anxiety on him because he cares for you.

1 Peter 5:7

God is not unjust; he will not forget your work and the love you have shown him as you have helped his people and continue to help them.

Hebrews 6:10

By standing firm you will gain life.

Luke 21:19

Not only so, but we also rejoice in our sufferings, because we know that suffering produces perseverance; perseverance, character; and character, hope.

And hope does not disappoint us, because God has poured out his love into our hearts by the Holy Spirit, whom he has given us.

Romans 5:3-5

"Therefore I tell you, do not worry about your life, what you will eat or drink; or about your body, what you will wear. Is not life more important than food, and the body more important than clothes?

Therefore do not worry about tomorrow, for tomorrow will worry about itself. Each day has enough trouble of its own.

Matthew 6:25,34

I am not saying this because I am in need, for I have learned to be content whatever the circumstances.

I know what it is to be in need, and I know what it is to have plenty. I have learned the secret of being content in any and every situation, whether well fed or hungry, whether living in plenty or in want.

Philippians 3:11 -12

In the same way, the Spirit helps us in our weakness. We do not know what we ought to pray for, but the Spirit himself intercedes for us with groans that words cannot express.

And he who searches our hearts knows the mind of the Spirit, because the Spirit intercedes for the saints in accordance with God's will.

Romans 8:26,27

THE ATHLETE'S TOPICAL BIBLE

The LORD will grant that the enemies who rise up against you will be defeated before you. They will come at you from one direction but flee from you in seven.

Deuteronomy 28:7

Be strong and courageous. Do not be afraid or terrified because of them, for the LORD your God goes with you; he will never leave you nor forsake you."

Deuteronomy 31:6

"Be strong and courageous, because you will lead these people to inherit the land I swore to their forefathers to give them.

Joshua 1:6

"The LORD has driven out before you great and powerful nations; to this day no one has been able to withstand you.

Joshua 23:9

If a man is lazy, the rafters sag; if his hands are idle, the house leaks.

Ecclesiastes 10:18

For I am the LORD, your God, who takes hold of your right hand and says to you, Do not fear; I will help you.

Isaiah 41:13

Laziness brings on deep sleep, and the shiftless man goes hungry.

Proverbs 19:15

"Ask and it will be given to you; seek and you will find; knock and the door will be opened to you. For everyone who asks receives; he who seeks finds; and to him who knocks, the door will be opened.

Matthew 7:7,8

But you will receive power when the Holy Spirit comes on you; and you will be my witnesses in Jerusalem, and in all Judea and Samaria, and to the ends of the earth."

Acts 1:8

The weapons we fight with are not the weapons of the world. On the contrary, they have divine power to demolish strongholds.

2 Corinthians 10:4

I can do everything through him who gives me strength.

Philippians 4:13

Diligent hands will rule, but laziness ends in slave labor.

Proverbs 12:24

Do you see a man skilled in his work? He will serve before kings; he will not serve before obscure men.

Proverbs 22:29

Never be lacking in zeal, but keep your spiritual fervor, serving the Lord.

Romans 12:11

He who gathers crops in summer is a wise son, but he who sleeps during harvest is a disgraceful son.

Proverbs 10:5

He who works his land will have abundant food, but he who chases fantasies lacks judgment.

Proverbs 12:11

We do not want you to become lazy, but to imitate those who through faith and patience inherit what has been promised.

Hebrews 6:12

If a man is lazy, the rafters sag; if his hands are idle, the house leaks.

Ecclesiastes 10:18

Therefore, I urge you, brothers, in view of God's mercy, to offer your bodies as living sacrifices, holy and pleasing to God —this is your spiritual act of worship.

Romans 12:1

But by the grace of God I am what I am, and his grace to me was not without effect. No, I worked harder than all of them —yet not I, but the grace of God that was with me.

1 Corinthians 15:10

"For God so loved the world that he gave his one and only Son, that whoever believes in him shall not perish but have eternal life.

John 3:16

The Athlete's Topical Bible

For God did not give us a spirit of timidity, but a spirit of power, of love and of self-discipline.

2 Timothy 1:7

Go to the ant, you sluggard; consider its ways and be wise! How long will you lie there, you sluggard? When will you get up from your sleep?

Proverbs 6:6,9

The sluggard craves and gets nothing, but the desires of the diligent are fully satisfied.

Proverbs 13:4

The sluggard is wiser in his own eyes than seven men who answer discreetly.

Proverbs 26:16

Have nothing to do with godless myths and old wives' tales; rather, train yourself to be godly.

For physical training is of some value, but godliness has value for all things, holding promise for both the present life and the life to come.

1 Timothy 4:7,8

Be strong and courageous. Do not be afraid or terrified because of them, for the LORD your God goes with you; he will never leave you nor forsake you."

Deuteronomy 31:6

"Come to me, all you who are weary and burdened, and I will give you rest.

Matthew 11:28

Above all else, guard your heart, for it is the wellspring of life

Proverbs 4:23

What, then, shall we say in response to this? If God is for us, who can be against us?

Romans 8:31

So we say with confidence, "The Lord is my helper; I will not be afraid. What can man do to me?"

Hebrews 13:6

Do not repay anyone evil for evil. Be careful to do what is right in the eyes of everybody.

Romans 12:17

A righteous man may have many troubles, but the LORD delivers him from them all.

Psalm 34:19

Find rest, O my soul, in God alone; my hope comes from him.

Psalm 62:5

Trust in the LORD with all your heart and lean not on your own understanding; in all your ways acknowledge him, and he will make your paths straight.

Proverbs 3:5,6

As for God, his way is perfect; the word of the LORD is flawless. He is a shield for all who take refuge in him.

Psalm 18:30

Be still before the LORD and wait patiently for him; do not fret when men succeed in their ways, when they carry out their wicked schemes.

Psalm 37:7

I sought the LORD, and he answered me; he delivered me from all my fears.

Those who look to him are radiant; their faces are never covered with shame.

Psalm 34:4,5

Why are you downcast, O my soul? Why so disturbed within me? Put your hope in God, for I will yet praise him, my Savior and my God.

Psalm 42:11

But I tell you: Love your enemies and pray for those who persecute you.

Matthew 5:44

Bless those who curse you, pray for those who mistreat you.

Luke 6:28

For the LORD your God detests anyone who does these things, anyone who deals dishonestly.

Deuteronomy 25:16

I will maintain my righteousness and never let go of it; my conscience will not reproach me as long as I live.

Job 27:6

For we are taking pains to do what is right, not only in the eyes of the Lord but also in the eyes of men.

2 Corinthians 8:21

My son, if sinners entice you, do not give in to them.my son, do not go along with them, do not set foot on their paths.

Proverbs 1:10,15

The LORD detests lying lips, but he delights in men who are truthful.

Proverbs 12:22

So I strive always to keep my conscience clear before God and man.

Acts 24:16

Pray for us. We are sure that we have a clear conscience and desire to live honorably in every way.

Hebrews 13:18

"Watch and pray so that you will not fall into temptation. The spirit is willing, but the body is weak."

Matthew 26:41

THE ATHLETE'S TOPICAL BIBLE

26

He who walks righteously and speaks what is right, who rejects gain from extortion and keeps his hand from accepting bribes, who stops his ears against plots of murder and shuts his eyes against contemplating evil--this is the man who will dwell on the heights, whose refuge will be the mountain fortress. His bread will be supplied, and water will not fail him.

Isaiah 33:15,16

Do to others as you would have them do to you.

Luke 6:31

Rather, we have renounced secret and shameful ways; we do not use deception, nor do we distort the word of God. On the contrary, by setting forth the truth plainly we commend ourselves to every man's conscience in the sight of God.

2 Corinthians 4:2

He who has clean hands and a pure heart, who does not lift up his soul to an idol or swear by what is false.

Psalm 24:4

Live such good lives among the pagans that, though they accuse you of doing wrong, they may see your good deeds and glorify God on the day he visits us.

1 Peter 2:12

No temptation has seized you except what is common to man. And God is faithful; he will not let you be tempted beyond what you can bear. But when you are tempted, he will also provide a way out so that you can stand up under it.

1 Corinthians 10:13

But if from there you seek the LORD your God, you will find him if you look for him with all your heart and with all your soul.

When you are in distress and all these things have happened to you, then in later days you will return to the LORD your God and obey him.

Deuteronomy 4:29,30

Be strong and courageous. Do not be afraid or terrified because of them, for the LORD your God goes with you; he will never leave you nor forsake you."

Deuteronomy 31:6

He replied, "Because you have so little faith. I tell you the truth, if you have faith as small as a mustard seed, you can say to this mountain, `Move from here to there' and it will move. Nothing will be impossible for you. "

Matthew 17:20

Do not let this Book of the Law depart from your mouth; meditate on it day and night, so that you may be careful to do everything written in it. Then you will be prosperous and successful.

Have I not commanded you? Be strong and courageous. Do not be terrified; do not be discouraged, for the LORD your God will be with you wherever you go."

Joshua 1:8,9

Since you are my rock and my fortress, for the sake of your name lead and guide me.

Psalm 31:3

THE ATHLETE'S TOPICAL BIBLE

28

David also said to Solomon his son, "Be strong and courageous, and do the work. Do not be afraid or discouraged, for the LORD God, my God, is with you. He will not fail you or forsake you until all the work for the service of the temple of the LORD is finished.

1 Chronicles 28:20

When I am afraid, I will trust in you.

In God, whose word I praise, in God I trust; I will not be afraid. What can mortal man do to me?

Psalm 56:3,4

I can do everything through him who gives me strength.

Philippians 4:13

A righteous man may have many troubles, but the LORD delivers him from them all.

Psalm 34:19

Jesus replied, "What is impossible with men is possible with God."

Luke 18:27

With God we will gain the victory, and he will trample down our enemies.

Psalm 60:12

With God we will gain the victory, and he will trample down our enemies.

Psalm 108:13

Jesus looked at them and said, "With man this is impossible, but with God all things are possible."

Matthew 19:26

29

THE ATHLETE'S TOPICAL BIBLE

But if from there you seek the LORD your God, you will find him if you look for him with all your heart and with all your soul.

When you are in distress and all these things have happened to you, then in later days you will return to the LORD your God and obey him.

For the LORD your God is a merciful God; he will not abandon or destroy you or forget the covenant with your forefathers, which he confirmed to them by oath.

Deuteronomy 4:29-31

Brothers, I do not consider myself yet to have taken hold of it. But one thing I do: Forgetting what is behind and straining toward what is ahead,

I press on toward the goal to win the prize for which God has called me heavenward in Christ Jesus.

Philippians 3:13,14

These have come so that your faith --of greater worth than gold, which perishes even though refined by fire --may be proved genuine and may result in praise, glory and honor when Jesus Christ is revealed.

1 Peter 1:7

He restores my soul. He guides me in paths of righteousness for his name's sake.

Psalm 23:3

Wait for the LORD; be strong and take heart and wait for the LORD.

Psalm 27:14

We are hard pressed on every side, but not crushed; perplexed, but not in despair; persecuted, but not abandoned; struck down, but not destroyed.

2 Corinthians 4:8,9

He who conceals his sins does not prosper, but whoever confesses and renounces them finds mercy.

Proverbs 28:13

So do not fear, for I am with you; do not be dismayed, for I am your God. I will strengthen you and help you; I will uphold you with my righteous right hand.

Isaiah 41:10

And we know that in all things God works for the good of those who love him, who have been called according to his purpose.

Romans 8:28

Cast all your anxiety on him because he cares for you.

1 Peter 5:7

If we confess our sins, he is faithful and just and will forgive us our sins and purify us from all unrighteousness.

1 John 1:9

He who conceals his sins does not prosper, but whoever confesses and renounces them finds mercy.

Proverbs 28:13

Trust in the LORD with all your heart and lean not on your own understanding; in all your ways acknowledge him, and he will make your paths straight.

Proverbs 3:5,6

My dear brothers, take note of this: Everyone should be quick to listen, slow to speak and slow to become angry, for man's anger does not bring about the righteous life that God desires.

James 1:19,20

Do not be quickly provoked in your spirit, for anger resides in the lap of fools.

Ecclesiastes 7:9

Likewise the tongue is a small part of the body, but it makes great boasts. Consider what a great forest is set on fire by a small spark.

James 3:5

But now you must rid yourselves of all such things as these: anger, rage, malice, slander, and filthy language from your lips.

Colossians 3:8

My lips will not speak wickedness, and my tongue will utter no deceit.

Job 27:4

Save me, O LORD, from lying lips and from deceitful tongues.

What will he do to you, and what more besides, O deceitful tongue?

Psalm 120:2,3

Resentment kills a fool, and envy slays the simple.

Job 5:2

THE ATHLETE'S TOPICAL BIBLE

Set a guard over my mouth, O LORD; keep watch over the door of my lips.

Psalm 141:3

When words are many, sin is not absent, but he who holds his tongue is wise.

Proverbs 10:19

A fool shows his annoyance at once, but a prudent man overlooks an insult.

Proverbs 12:16

He who guards his lips guards his life, but he who speaks rashly will come to ruin.

Proverbs 13:3

A patient man has great understanding, but a quick-tempered man displays folly.

Proverbs 14:29

A gentle answer turns away wrath, but a harsh word stirs up anger.

Proverbs 15:1

"In your anger do not sin" : Do not let the sun go down while you are still angry.

Ephesians 4:26

Not only so, but we also rejoice in our sufferings, because A gentle answer turns away wrath, but a harsh word stirs up anger.

Proverbs 15:1

THE ATHLETE'S TOPICAL BIBLE

Do not be anxious about anything, but in everything, by prayer and petition, with thanksgiving, present your requests to God.

And the peace of God, which transcends all understanding, will guard your hearts and your minds in Christ Jesus.

Philippians 4:6,7

I can do everything through him who gives me strength.

And my God will meet all your needs according to his glorious riches in Christ Jesus.

Philippians 4:13,19

Love is patient, love is kind. It does not envy, it does not boast, it is not proud.

It is not rude, it is not self-seeking, it is not easily angered, it keeps no record of wrongs.

1 Corinthians 13:4,5

But the fruit of the Spirit is love, joy, peace, patience, kindness, goodness, faithfulness, gentleness and self-control. Against such things there is no law.

Galatians 5:22,23

Not only so, but we also rejoice in our sufferings, because we know that suffering produces perseverance; perseverance, character; and character, hope.

And hope does not disappoint us, because God has poured out his love into our hearts by the Holy Spirit, whom he has given us.

Romans 5:3-5

I have been crucified with Christ and I no longer live, but Christ lives in me. The life I live in the body, I live by faith in the Son of God, who loved me and gave himself for me.

Galatians 2:20

Be patient, then, brothers, until the Lord's coming. See how the farmer waits for the land to yield its valuable crop and how patient he is for the autumn and spring rains.

You too, be patient and stand firm, because the Lord's coming is near.

James 5:7,8

Be still before the LORD and wait patiently for him; do not fret when men succeed in their ways, when they carry out their wicked schemes.

Psalm 37:7

For this very reason, make every effort to add to your faith goodness; and to goodness, knowledge; and to knowledge, self-control; and to self-control, perseverance; and to perseverance, godliness; and to godliness, brotherly kindness; and to brotherly kindness, love.

For if you possess these qualities in increasing measure, they will keep you from being ineffective and unproductive in your knowledge of our Lord Jesus Christ.

But if anyone does not have them, he is nearsighted and blind, and has forgotten that he has been cleansed from his past sins.

2 Peter 1:5-9

Be completely humble and gentle; be patient, bearing with one another in love.

Ephesians 4:2

35

I can do everything through him who gives me strength.

Philippians 4:13

Each one should use whatever gift he has received to serve others, faithfully administering God's grace in its various forms.

If anyone speaks, he should do it as one speaking the very words of God. If anyone serves, he should do it with the strength God provides, so that in all things God may be praised through Jesus Christ. To him be the glory and the power for ever and ever. Amen.

1 Peter 4:10,11

And I have filled him with the Spirit of God, with skill, ability and knowledge in all kinds of crafts.

Exodus 31:3

Grace and peace be yours in abundance through the knowledge of God and of Jesus our Lord.

His divine power has given us everything we need for life and godliness through our knowledge of him who called us by his own glory and goodness.

2 Peter 1:2,3

Praise be to the LORD my Rock, who trains my hands for war, my fingers for battle.

Psalm 144:1

With your help I can advance against a troop; with my God I can scale a wall.

Psalm 18:29

The Athlete's Topical Bible

36

And my God will meet all your needs according to his glorious riches in Christ Jesus.

Philippians 4:19

But thanks be to God! He gives us the victory through our Lord Jesus Christ.

1 Corinthians 15:57

Are not two sparrows sold for a penny? Yet not one of them will fall to the ground apart from the will of your Father.

And even the very hairs of your head are all numbered.

So don't be afraid; you are worth more than many sparrows.

Matthew 10:29-31

Never be lacking in zeal, but keep your spiritual fervor, serving the Lord.

Romans 12:11

Diligent hands will rule, but laziness ends in slave labor.

Proverbs 12:24

The LORD is my strength and my song; he has become my salvation. He is my God, and I will praise him, my father's God, and I will exalt him.

Exodus 15:2

Finally, be strong in the Lord and in his mighty power.

Ephesians 6:10

The LORD is my strength and my song; he has become my salvation.

Psalm 118:14

THE ATHLETE'S TOPICAL BIBLE

Have I not commanded you? Be strong and courageous. Do not be terrified; do not be discouraged, for the LORD your God will be with you wherever you go."

Joshua 1:9

I press on toward the goal to win the prize for which God has called me heavenward in Christ Jesus.

Philippians 3:14

But as for you, be strong and do not give up, for your work will be rewarded."

2 Chronicles 15:7

For you have been my hope, O Sovereign LORD, my confidence since my youth.

Psalm 71:5

So do not throw away your confidence; it will be richly rewarded.

Hebrews 10:35

I can do everything through him who gives me strength.

Philippians 4:13

He replied, "If you have faith as small as a mustard seed, you can say to this mulberry tree, `Be uprooted and planted in the sea,' and it will obey you.

Luke 17:6

"`If you can'?" said Jesus. "Everything is possible for him who believes."

Mark 9:23

"But blessed is the man who trusts in the LORD, whose confidence is in him.

He will be like a tree planted by the water that sends out its roots by the stream. It does not fear when heat comes; its leaves are always green. It has no worries in a year of drought and never fails to bear fruit."

Jeremiah 17:7,18

Not only so, but we also rejoice in our sufferings, because we know that suffering produces perseverance; perseverance, character; and character, hope.

And hope does not disappoint us, because God has poured out his love into our hearts by the Holy Spirit, whom he has given us.

Romans 5:3-5

May the God of hope fill you with all joy and peace as you trust in him, so that you may overflow with hope by the power of the Holy Spirit.

Romans 15:13

Good will come to him who is generous and lends freely, who conducts his affairs with justice. Surely he will never be shaken; a righteous man will be remembered forever.

He will have no fear of bad news; his heart is steadfast, trusting in the LORD.

Psalm 112:5-7

Trust in the LORD with all your heart and lean not on your own understanding; in all your ways acknowledge him, and he will make your paths straight.

Proverbs 3:5,6

A man's wisdom gives him patience; it is to his glory to overlook an offense.

Proverbs 19:11

Like a city whose walls are broken down is a man who lacks self-control.

Proverbs 25:28

The end of a matter is better than its beginning, and patience is better than pride. Do not be quickly provoked in your spirit, for anger resides in the lap of fools.

Ecclesiastes 7:8,9

Do to others as you would have them do to you.

Luke 6:31

To those who by persistence in doing good seek glory, honor and immortality, he will give eternal life.

Romans 2:7

Let us not become weary in doing good, for at the proper time we will reap a harvest if we do not give up.

Galatians 6:9

Do not be anxious about anything, but in everything, by prayer and petition, with thanksgiving, present your requests to God.

Philippians 4:6

For it is commendable if a man bears up under the pain of unjust suffering because he is conscious of God.

1 Peter 2:19

Keep me as the apple of your eye; hide me in the shadow of your wings.

Psalm 17:8

You are my hiding place; you will protect me from trouble and surround me with songs of deliverance. Selah

Psalm 32:7

Hide me from the conspiracy of the wicked, from that noisy crowd of evildoers.

Psalm 64:2

You are my refuge and my shield; I have put my hope in your word.

Psalm 119:114

Rescue me from my enemies, O LORD, for I hide myself in you.

Psalm 143:9

To do what is right and just is more acceptable to the LORD than sacrifice.

Proverbs 21:3

There is a time for everything, and a season for every activity under heaven:
A time to tear and a time to mend, a time to be silent and a time to speak.

Ecclesiastes 3:1,7

Bless those who curse you, pray for those who mistreat you.

Luke 6:28

41

THE ATHLETE'S TOPICAL BIBLE

So in everything, do to others what you would have them do to you, for this sums up the Law and the Prophets.

Matthew 7:12

And the second is like it: `Love your neighbor as yourself.'

Matthew 22:39

By this all men will know that you are my disciples, if you love one another."

John 13:35

Rejoice with those who rejoice; mourn with those who mourn.

Romans 12:15

We who are strong ought to bear with the failings of the weak and not to please ourselves.

Romans 15:1

If you really keep the royal law found in Scripture, "Love your neighbor as yourself," you are doing right.

James 2:8

Therefore encourage one another and build each other up, just as in fact you are doing

1 Thessalonians 5:11

Do not withhold good from those who deserve it, when it is in your power to act.

Do not say to your neighbor, "Come back later; I'll give it tomorrow"-- when you now have it with you.

Proverbs 3:27,28

42

And we urge you, brothers, warn those who are idle, encourage the timid, help the weak, be patient with everyone.

1 Thessalonians 5:14

Praise be to the God and Father of our Lord Jesus Christ, the Father of compassion and the God of all comfort, who comforts us in all our troubles, so that we can comfort those in any trouble with the comfort we ourselves have received from God.

For just as the sufferings of Christ flow over into our lives, so also through Christ our comfort overflows.

2 Corinthians 1:3-5

Carry each other's burdens, and in this way you will fulfill the law of Christ.

Galatians 6:2

If you really keep the royal law found in Scripture, "Love your neighbor as yourself," you are doing right.

James 2:8

But encourage one another daily, as long as it is called Today, so that none of you may be hardened by sin's deceitfulness.

Hebrews 3:13

Pleasant words are a honeycomb, sweet to the soul and healing to the bones.

Proverbs 16:24

The Athlete's Topical Bible

Whatever you do, work at it with all your heart, as working for the Lord, not for men.

Colossians 3:23

For you have been my hope, O Sovereign LORD, my confidence since my youth.

Psalm 71:5

"`If you can'?" said Jesus. "Everything is possible for him who believes."

Mark 9:23

He replied, "If you have faith as small as a mustard seed, you can say to this mulberry tree, `Be uprooted and planted in the sea,' and it will obey you.

Luke 17:6

I press on toward the goal to win the prize for which God has called me heavenward in Christ Jesus.

Philippians 3:14

I can do everything through him who gives me strength.

Philippians 4:13

So do not throw away your confidence; it will be richly rewarded.

Hebrews 10:35

Diligent hands will rule, but laziness ends in slave labor.
The lazy man does not roast his game, but the diligent man prizes his possessions.

Proverbs 12:24,27

The sluggard craves and gets nothing, but the desires of the diligent are fully satisfied.

Proverbs 13:4

The plans of the diligent lead to profit as surely as haste leads to poverty.

Proverbs 21:5

Do you see a man skilled in his work? He will serve before kings; he will not serve before obscure men.

Proverbs 22:29

But the one who does not know and does things deserving punishment will be beaten with few blows. From everyone who has been given much, much will be demanded; and from the one who has been entrusted with much, much more will be asked.

Luke 12:48

Be very careful, then, how you live --not as unwise but as wise, making the most of every opportunity, because the days are evil.

Ephesians 5:15,16

And whatever you do, whether in word or deed, do it all in the name of the Lord Jesus, giving thanks to God the Father through him.

Colossians 3:17

Carry each other's burdens, and in this way you will fulfill the law of Christ.

Galatians 6:2

Dear friends, since God so loved us, we also ought to love one another.

1 John 4:11

Perfume and incense bring joy to the heart, and the pleasantness of one's friend springs from his earnest counsel.

Proverbs 27:9

As iron sharpens iron, so one man sharpens another.

Proverbs 27:17

Two are better than one, because they have a good return for their work:

If one falls down, his friend can help him up. But pity the man who falls and has no one to help him up!

Ecclesiastes 4:9,10

Therefore encourage one another and build each other up, just as in fact you are doing.

1 Thessalonians 5:11

A man of many companions may come to ruin, but there is a friend who sticks closer than a brother.

Proverbs 18:24

A friend loves at all times, and a brother is born for adversity.

Proverbs 17:17

THE ATHLETE'S TOPICAL BIBLE

Finally, all of you, live in harmony with one another; be sympathetic, love as brothers, be compassionate and humble.

1 Peter 3:8

But those who hope in the LORD will renew their strength. They will soar on wings like eagles; they will run and not grow weary, they will walk and not be faint.

Isaiah 40:31

So in everything, do to others what you would have them do to you, for this sums up the Law and the Prophets.

Matthew 7:12

"A new command I give you: Love one another. As I have loved you, so you must love one another.

John 13:34

In everything I did, I showed you that by this kind of hard work we must help the weak, remembering the words the Lord Jesus himself said: `It is more blessed to give than to receive.'"

Acts 20:35

That is, that you and I may be mutually encouraged by each other's faith.

Romans 1:12

And we urge you, brothers, warn those who are idle, encourage the timid, help the weak, be patient with everyone.

1 Thessalonians 5:14

THE ATHLETE'S TOPICAL BIBLE

Similarly, encourage the young men to be self-controlled.
Titus 2:6

But encourage one another daily, as long as it is called Today, so that none of you may be hardened by sin's deceitfulness.
Hebrews 3:13

Let us not give up meeting together, as some are in the habit of doing, but let us encourage one another --and all the more as you see the Day approaching.
Hebrews 10:25

Do nothing out of selfish ambition or vain conceit, but in humility consider others better than yourselves.
Each of you should look not only to your own interests, but also to the interests of others.
Philippians 2:3,4

Be completely humble and gentle; be patient, bearing with one another in love.
Ephesians 4:2

Perfume and incense bring joy to the heart, and the pleasantness of one's friend springs from his earnest counsel.
Proverbs 27:9

But as for you, be strong and do not give up, for your work will be rewarded."

2 Chronicles 15:7

I will instruct you and teach you in the way you should go; I will counsel you and watch over you.

Psalm 32:8

You guide me with your counsel, and afterward you will take me into glory.

Psalm 73:24

Trust in the LORD with all your heart and lean not on your own understanding.

Proverbs 3:5

Do you see a man skilled in his work? He will serve before kings; he will not serve before obscure men.

Proverbs 22:29

Strengthen the feeble hands, steady the knees that give way.

Isaiah 35:3

So do not fear, for I am with you; do not be dismayed, for I am your God. I will strengthen you and help you; I will uphold you with my righteous right hand.

Isaiah 41:10

But seek first his kingdom and his righteousness, and all these things will be given to you as well.

Matthew 6:33

Teach me your way, O LORD; lead me in a straight path because of my oppressors.

Psalm 27:11

My times are in your hands; deliver me from my enemies and from those who pursue me.

Let your face shine on your servant; save me in your unfailing love.

Psalm 31:15,16

The angel of the LORD encamps around those who fear him, and he delivers them.

Taste and see that the LORD is good; blessed is the man who takes refuge in him.

Psalm 34:7,8

Even my close friend, whom I trusted, he who shared my bread, has lifted up his heel against me.

But you, O LORD, have mercy on me; raise me up, that I may repay them.

I know that you are pleased with me, for my enemy does not triumph over me.

Psalm 41:9-11

Do not gloat over me, my enemy! Though I have fallen, I will rise. Though I sit in darkness, the LORD will be my light.

Micah 7:8

For you, O God, tested us; you refined us like silver.

Psalm 66:10

But the Lord stood at my side and gave me strength, so that through me the message might be fully proclaimed and all the Gentiles might hear it. And I was delivered from the lion's mouth.

2 Timothy 4:17

Keeping a clear conscience, so that those who speak maliciously against your good behavior in Christ may be ashamed of their slander.

1 Peter 3:16

Get rid of all bitterness, rage and anger, brawling and slander, along with every form of malice.

Ephesians 4:31

Therefore, my dear brothers, stand firm. Let nothing move you. Always give yourselves fully to the work of the Lord, because you know that your labor in the Lord is not in vain.

1 Corinthians 15:58

Being confident of this, that he who began a good work in you will carry it on to completion until the day of Christ Jesus.

Philippians 1:6

For it is God who works in you to will and to act according to his good purpose.

Philippians 2:13

So don't be afraid; you are worth more than many sparrows.

Matthew 10:31

"Be still, and know that I am God; I will be exalted among the nations, I will be exalted in the earth."

Psalm 46:10

My flesh and my heart may fail, but God is the strength of my heart and my portion forever.

Psalm 73:26

Though I walk in the midst of trouble, you preserve my life; you stretch out your hand against the anger of my foes, with your right hand you save me.

The LORD will fulfill [his purpose] for me; your love, O LORD, endures forever-- do not abandon the works of your hands.

Psalm 138:7,8

If you falter in times of trouble, how small is your strength!

Proverbs 24:10

God is not unjust; he will not forget your work and the love you have shown him as you have helped his people and continue to help them.

Hebrews 6:10

I consider that our present sufferings are not worth comparing with the glory that will be revealed in us.

Romans 8:18

And we know that in all things God works for the good of those who love him, who have been called according to his purpose.

Romans 8:28

Dear friends, do not be surprised at the painful trial you are suffering, as though something strange were happening to you.

But rejoice that you participate in the sufferings of Christ, so that you may be overjoyed when his glory is revealed.

1 Peter 4:12,13

By standing firm you will gain life.

Luke 21:19

Not only so, but we also rejoice in our sufferings, because we know that suffering produces perseverance; perseverance, character; and character, hope.

And hope does not disappoint us, because God has poured out his love into our hearts by the Holy Spirit, whom he has given us.

Romans 5:3-5

We are hard pressed on every side, but not crushed; perplexed, but not in despair; persecuted, but not abandoned; struck down, but not destroyed.

2 Corinthians 4:8,9

Brothers, I do not consider myself yet to have taken hold of it. But one thing I do: Forgetting what is behind and straining toward what is ahead,

Philippians 3:13

THE ATHLETE'S TOPICAL BIBLE

However, if you suffer as a Christian, do not be ashamed, but praise God that you bear that name. So then, those who suffer according to God's will should commit themselves to their faithful Creator and continue to do good.

1 Peter 4:16,19

Consider it pure joy, my brothers, whenever you face trials of many kinds, because you know that the testing of your faith develops perseverance.

Perseverance must finish its work so that you may be mature and complete, not lacking anything. If any of you lacks wisdom, he should ask God, who gives generously to all without finding fault, and it will be given to him. But when he asks, he must believe and not doubt, because he who doubts is like a wave of the sea, blown and tossed by the wind. That man should not think he will receive anything from the Lord; he is a double-minded man, unstable in all he does.

The brother in humble circumstances ought to take pride in his high position. But the one who is rich should take pride in his low position, because he will pass away like a wild flower. For the sun rises with scorching heat and withers the plant; its blossom falls and its beauty is destroyed. In the same way, the rich man will fade away even while he goes about his business.

James 1:2-11

Trust in the LORD with all your heart and lean not on your own understanding; in all your ways acknowledge him, and he will make your paths straight.

Proverbs 3:5

Do not be anxious about anything, but in everything, by prayer and petition, with thanksgiving, present your requests to God. And the peace of God, which transcends all understanding, will guard your hearts and your minds in Christ Jesus.

Philippians 4:6,7

Who shall separate us from the love of Christ? Shall trouble or hardship or persecution or famine or nakedness or danger or sword?

No, in all these things we are more than conquerors through him who loved us.

Romans 8:35,37

"Do not let your hearts be troubled. Trust in God; trust also in me.

John 14:1

But he said to me, "My grace is sufficient for you, for my power is made perfect in weakness." Therefore I will boast all the more gladly about my weaknesses, so that Christ's power may rest on me.

2 Corinthians 12:9

Yet man is born to trouble as surely as sparks fly upward.

Job 5:7

"I have told you these things, so that in me you may have peace. In this world you will have trouble. But take heart! I have overcome the world."

John 16:33

I can do everything through him who gives me strength.

Philippians 4:13

55

THE ATHLETE'S TOPICAL BIBLE

Everyone must submit himself to the governing authorities, for there is no authority except that which God has established. The authorities that exist have been established by God.

Romans 13:1

Remind the people to be subject to rulers and authorities, to be obedient, to be ready to do whatever is good.

Titus 3:1

Who is going to harm you if you are eager to do good?

But even if you should suffer for what is right, you are blessed. "Do not fear what they fear; do not be frightened."

1 Peter 3:13,14

Hold them in the highest regard in love because of their work. Live in peace with each other.

And we urge you, brothers, warn those who are idle, encourage the timid, help the weak, be patient with everyone.

1 Thessalonians 5:13,14

Submit to one another out of reverence for Christ.

Ephesians 5:21

Slaves, obey your earthly masters with respect and fear, and with sincerity of heart, just as you would obey Christ.

Obey them not only to win their favor when their eye is on you, but like slaves of Christ, doing the will of God from your heart.

Ephesians 6:5,6

"No one can serve two masters. Either he will hate the one and love the other, or he will be devoted to the one and despise the other. You cannot serve both God and Money.

Matthew 6:24

For the love of money is a root of all kinds of evil. Some people, eager for money, have wandered from the faith and pierced themselves with many griefs.

1 Timothy 6:10

Then some soldiers asked him, "And what should we do?" He replied, "Don't extort money and don't accuse people falsely --be content with your pay."

Luke 3:14

Keep your lives free from the love of money and be content with what you have, because God has said, "Never will I leave you; never will I forsake you."

Hebrews 13:5

For by the grace given me I say to every one of you: Do not think of yourself more highly than you ought, but rather think of yourself with sober judgment, in accordance with the measure of faith God has given you.

Romans 12:3

Do not be anxious about anything, but in everything, by prayer and petition, with thanksgiving, present your requests to God.

Philippians 4:6

If anyone does not provide for his relatives, and especially for his immediate family, he has denied the faith and is worse than an unbeliever.

1 Timothy 5:8

THE ATHLETE'S TOPICAL BIBLE

For it is not the one who commends himself who is approved, but the one whom the Lord commends.

2 Corinthians 10:18

For by the grace given me I say to every one of you: Do not think of yourself more highly than you ought, but rather think of yourself with sober judgment, in accordance with the measure of faith God has given you.

Romans 12:3

How can you believe if you accept praise from one another, yet make no effort to obtain the praise that comes from the only God?

John 5:44

Let another praise you, and not your own mouth; someone else, and not your own lips.

Proverbs 27:2

He mocks proud mockers but gives grace to the humble.

Proverbs 3:34

Now I, Nebuchadnezzar, praise and exalt and glorify the King of heaven, because everything he does is right and all his ways are just. And those who walk in pride he is able to humble.

Daniel 4:37

Therefore, as God's chosen people, holy and dearly loved, clothe yourselves with compassion, kindness, humility, gentleness and patience.

Colossians 3:12

Young men, in the same way be submissive to those who are older. All of you, clothe yourselves with humility toward one another, because, "God opposes the proud but gives grace to the humble."

1 Peter 5:5

The fear of the LORD teaches a man wisdom, and humility comes before honor.

Proverbs 15:33

Before his downfall a man's heart is proud, but humility comes before honor.

Proverbs 18:12

Humility and the fear of the LORD bring wealth and honor and life.

Proverbs 22:4

Do nothing out of selfish ambition or vain conceit, but in humility consider others better than yourselves.

Philippians 2:3

Has not my hand made all these things, and so they came into being?" declares the LORD. "This is the one I esteem: he who is humble and contrite in spirit, and trembles at my word.

Isaiah 66:2

A man's pride brings him low, but a man of lowly spirit gains honor.

Proverbs 29:23

Humble yourselves before the Lord, and he will lift you up.

James 4:10

THE ATHLETE'S TOPICAL BIBLE

Y ou became imitators of us and of the Lord; in spite of severe suffering, you welcomed the message with the joy given by the Holy Spirit.

And so you became a model to all the believers in Macedonia and Achaia.

1 Thessalonians 1:6,7

Follow my example, as I follow the example of Christ.

1 Corinthians 11:1

"Be strong and courageous, because you will lead these people to inherit the land I swore to their forefathers to give them.

Joshua 1:6

Don't let anyone look down on you because you are young, but set an example for the believers in speech, in life, in love, in faith and in purity.

1 Timothy 4:12

Not lording it over those entrusted to you, but being examples to the flock.

1 Peter 5:3

Not so with you. Instead, whoever wants to become great among you must be your servant.

Matthew 20:26

Be shepherds of God's flock that is under your care, serving as overseers --not because you must, but because you are willing, as God wants you to be; not greedy for money, but eager to serve.

1 Peter 5:2

Refrain from anger and turn from wrath; do not fret --it leads only to evil.

Psalm 37:8

Get rid of all bitterness, rage and anger, brawling and slander, along with every form of malice.

Ephesians 4:31

My dear brothers, take note of this: Everyone should be quick to listen, slow to speak and slow to become angry, for man's anger does not bring about the righteous life that God desires.

James 1:19,20

Better a patient man than a warrior, a man who controls his temper than one who takes a city.

Proverbs 16:32

In your anger do not sin; when you are on your beds, search your hearts and be silent. Selah

Psalm 4:4

"In your anger do not sin" : Do not let the sun go down while you are still angry, and do not give the devil a foothold.

Ephesians 4:26,27

You were taught, with regard to your former way of life, to put off your old self, which is being corrupted by its deceitful desires; to be made new in the attitude of your minds; and to put on the new self, created to be like God in true righteousness and holiness.

Ephesians 4:22-24

61

THE ATHLETE'S TOPICAL BIBLE

Refrain from anger and turn from wrath; do not fret --it leads only to evil.

Psalm 37:8

O LORD, the God who avenges, O God who avenges, shine forth.

Psalm 94:1

Do not take revenge, my friends, but leave room for God's wrath, for it is written: "It is mine to avenge; I will repay," says the Lord.

Romans 12:19

A fool gives full vent to his anger, but a wise man keeps himself under control.

Proverbs 29:11

My dear brothers, take note of this: Everyone should be quick to listen, slow to speak and slow to become angry, for man's anger does not bring about the righteous life that God desires.

James 1:19,20

A gentle answer turns away wrath, but a harsh word stirs up anger.

Proverbs 15:1

But now you must rid yourselves of all such things as these: anger, rage, malice, slander, and filthy language from your lips.

Colossians 3:8

A fool gives full vent to his anger, but a wise man keeps himself under control.

Proverbs 29:11

"In your anger do not sin" : Do not let the sun go down while you are still angry, and do not give the devil a foothold.

Ephesians 4:26,27

A quick-tempered man does foolish things, and a crafty man is hated.

Proverbs 14:17

Better a patient man than a warrior, a man who controls his temper than one who takes a city.

Proverbs 16:32

Do not be quickly provoked in your spirit, for anger resides in the lap of fools.

Ecclesiastes 7:9

My dear brothers, take note of this: Everyone should be quick to listen, slow to speak and slow to become angry.

James 1:19

Do not repay evil with evil or insult with insult, but with blessing, because to this you were called so that you may inherit a blessing.

1 Peter 3:9

The Athlete's Topical Bible

So Jacob was left alone, and a man wrestled with him till daybreak. When the man saw that he could not overpower him, he touched the socket of Jacob's hip so that his hip was wrenched as he wrestled with the man.

Genesis 32:24-25

Among all these soldiers there were seven hundred chosen men who were left-handed, each of whom could sling a stone at a hair and not miss.

Judges 20:16

Therefore I do not run like a man running aimlessly; I do not fight like a man beating the air.

1 Corinthians 9:26

Everyone who competes in the games goes into strict training. They do it to get a crown that will not last; but we do it to get a crown that will last forever.

1 Corinthians 9:25

For our struggle is not against flesh and blood, but against the rulers, against the authorities, against the powers of this dark world and against the spiritual forces of evil in the heavenly realms.

Ephesians 6:12

Brothers, I do not consider myself yet to have taken hold of it. But one thing I do: Forgetting what is behind and straining toward what is ahead, I press on toward the goal to win the prize for which God has called me heavenward in Christ Jesus.

Philippians 3:13,14

Therefore, since we are surrounded by such a great cloud of witnesses, let us throw off everything that hinders and the sin that so easily entangles, and let us run with perseverance the race marked out for us.

Let us fix our eyes on Jesus, the author and perfecter of our faith, who for the joy set before him endured the cross, scorning its shame, and sat down at the right hand of the throne of God.

Hebrews 12:1,2

I went in response to a revelation and set before them the gospel that I preach among the Gentiles. But I did this privately to those who seemed to be leaders, for fear that I was running or had run my race in vain.

Galatians 2:2

As you hold out the word of life --in order that I may boast on the day of Christ that I did not run or labor for nothing.

Philippians 2:16

I run in the path of your commands, for you have set my heart free.

Psalm 119:32

Now there is in store for me the crown of righteousness, which the Lord, the righteous Judge, will award to me on that day --and not only to me, but also to all who have longed for his appearing.

2 Timothy 4:8

THE ATHLETE'S TOPICAL BIBLE

Do you not know that in a race all the runners run, but only one gets the prize? Run in such a way as to get the prize.

Everyone who competes in the games goes into strict training. They do it to get a crown that will not last; but we do it to get a crown that will last forever.

Therefore I do not run like a man running aimlessly; I do not fight like a man beating the air.

No, I beat my body and make it my slave so that after I have preached to others, I myself will not be disqualified for the prize.

1 Corinthians 9:24-27

Similarly, if anyone competes as an athlete, he does not receive the victor's crown unless he competes according to the rules.

2 Timothy 2:5

Everyone who competes in the games goes into strict training. They do it to get a crown that will not last; but we do it to get a crown that will last forever.

1 Corinthians 9:25

And when the Chief Shepherd appears, you will receive the crown of glory that will never fade away.

1 Peter 5:4

OFF THE COURT

Quarter

THE ATHLETE'S TOPICAL BIBLE

Blessed are those who are persecuted because of righteousness, for theirs is the kingdom of heaven.

"Blessed are you when people insult you, persecute you and falsely say all kinds of evil against you because of me.

Rejoice and be glad, because great is your reward in heaven, for in the same way they persecuted the prophets who were before you.

Matthew 5:10-12

A righteous man may have many troubles, but the LORD delivers him from them all.

Psalm 34:19

The apostles left the Sanhedrin, rejoicing because they had been counted worthy of suffering disgrace for the Name.

Acts 5:41

He chose to be mistreated along with the people of God rather than to enjoy the pleasures of sin for a short time.

Hebrews 11:25

O LORD, see how my enemies persecute me! Have mercy and lift me up from the gates of death.

Psalm 9:13

Many are the foes who persecute me, but I have not turned from your statutes.

Psalm 119:157

Bless those who persecute you; bless and do not curse.

Romans 12:14

But how is it to your credit if you receive a beating for doing wrong and endure it? But if you suffer for doing good and you endure it, this is commendable before God.

1 Peter 2:20

Do not be surprised, my brothers, if the world hates you.

1 John 3:13

All this is evidence that God's judgment is right, and as a result you will be counted worthy of the kingdom of God, for which you are suffering.

God is just: He will pay back trouble to those who trouble you

2 Thessalonians 1:5,6

Fear of man will prove to be a snare, but whoever trusts in the LORD is kept safe.

Proverbs 29:25

But I tell you: Love your enemies and pray for those who persecute you.

Matthew 5:44

Remember the words I spoke to you: `No servant is greater than his master.' If they persecuted me, they will persecute you also. If they obeyed my teaching, they will obey yours also.

John 15:20

"Blessed are you when people insult you, persecute you and falsely say all kinds of evil against you because of me.

Matthew 5:11

THE **A**THLETE'S **T**OPICAL **B**IBLE

Have nothing to do with the fruitless deeds of darkness, but rather expose them.

For it is shameful even to mention what the disobedient do in secret.

Ephesians 5:11,12

Finally, brothers, whatever is true, whatever is noble, whatever is right, whatever is pure, whatever is lovely, whatever is admirable --if anything is excellent or praiseworthy --think about such things.

Whatever you have learned or received or heard from me, or seen in me --put it into practice. And the God of peace will be with you.

Philippians 4:8,9

Turn my eyes away from worthless things; preserve my life according to your word.

Psalm 119:37

I will set before my eyes no vile thing. The deeds of faithless men I hate; they will not cling to me.

Psalm 101:3

Do not love the world or anything in the world. If anyone loves the world, the love of the Father is not in him.

For everything in the world --the cravings of sinful man, the lust of his eyes and the boasting of what he has and does --comes not from the Father but from the world.

The world and its desires pass away, but the man who does the will of God lives forever.

1 John 2:15-17

Therefore, my dear friends, as you have always obeyed -- not only in my presence, but now much more in my absence --continue to work out your salvation with fear and trembling, for it is God who works in you to will and to act according to his good purpose.

Do everything without complaining or arguing.

Philippians 2:12-14

Because anyone who serves Christ in this way is pleasing to God and approved by men.

Let us therefore make every effort to do what leads to peace and to mutual edification.

Romans 14:18,19

Since, then, you have been raised with Christ, set your hearts on things above, where Christ is seated at the right hand of God.

Set your minds on things above, not on earthly things.

And whatever you do, whether in word or deed, do it all in the name of the Lord Jesus, giving thanks to God the Father through him.

Colossians 3:1,2,17

Let us therefore make every effort to do what leads to peace and to mutual edification.

It is better not to eat meat or drink wine or to do anything else that will cause your brother to fall.

Romans 14:19,21

Do not be hasty in the laying on of hands, and do not share in the sins of others. Keep yourself pure.

1 Timothy 5:22

But you are a shield around me, O LORD; you bestow glory on me and lift up my head.

Psalm 3:3

Cast all your anxiety on him because he cares for you.

1 Peter 5:7

If this is so, then the Lord knows how to rescue godly men from trials and to hold the unrighteous for the day of judgment, while continuing their punishment.

2 Peter 2:9

But make up your mind not to worry beforehand how you will defend yourselves.

For I will give you words and wisdom that none of your adversaries will be able to resist or contradict.

Luke 21:14,15

The LORD is a refuge for the oppressed, a stronghold in times of trouble.

Psalm 9:9

He gives strength to the weary and increases the power of the weak.

But those who hope in the LORD will renew their strength. They will soar on wings like eagles; they will run and not grow weary, they will walk and not be faint.

Isaiah 40:29,31

In vain you rise early and stay up late, toiling for food to eat-- for he grants sleep to those he loves.

Psalm 127:2

THE ATHLETE'S TOPICAL BIBLE

So do not fear, for I am with you; do not be dismayed, for I am your God. I will strengthen you and help you; I will uphold you with my righteous right hand.

Isaiah 41:10

I love you, O LORD, my strength.

The LORD is my rock, my fortress and my deliverer; my God is my rock, in whom I take refuge. He is my shield and the horn of my salvation, my stronghold.

Psalm 18:1,2

Though an army besiege me, my heart will not fear; though war break out against me, even then will I be confident.

For in the day of trouble he will keep me safe in his dwelling; he will hide me in the shelter of his tabernacle and set me high upon a rock.

Psalm 27:3,5

My flesh and my heart may fail, but God is the strength of my heart and my portion forever.

Psalm 73:26

He sent forth his word and healed them; he rescued them from the grave.

Psalm 107:20

When you lie down, you will not be afraid; when you lie down, your sleep will be sweet.

Proverbs 3:24

He who fears the LORD has a secure fortress, and for his children it will be a refuge.

Proverbs 14:26

THE ATHLETE'S TOPICAL BIBLE

For if you forgive men when they sin against you, your heavenly Father will also forgive you.

Matthew 6:14

Bear with each other and forgive whatever grievances you may have against one another. Forgive as the Lord forgave you.

Colossians 3:13

"In your anger do not sin" : Do not let the sun go down while you are still angry, and do not give the devil a foothold.

Ephesians 4:26,27

"This is how my heavenly Father will treat each of you unless you forgive your brother from your heart."

Matthew 18:35

Be kind and compassionate to one another, forgiving each other, just as in Christ God forgave you.

Ephesians 4:32

Forgive us our debts, as we also have forgiven our debtors.

Matthew 6:12

Forgive us our sins, for we also forgive everyone who sins against us. And lead us not into temptation. '"

Luke 11:4

Then Peter came to Jesus and asked, "Lord, how many times shall I forgive my brother when he sins against me? Up to seven times?"

Jesus answered, "I tell you, not seven times, but seventy-seven times.

Matthew 18:21,22

So watch yourselves. "If your brother sins, rebuke him, and if he repents, forgive him.

Luke 17:3

A man's wisdom gives him patience; it is to his glory to overlook an offense.

Proverbs 19:11

Blessed are the merciful, for they will be shown mercy.

Matthew 5:7

Do not repay evil with evil or insult with insult, but with blessing, because to this you were called so that you may inherit a blessing.

1 Peter 3:9

But love your enemies, do good to them, and lend to them without expecting to get anything back. Then your reward will be great, and you will be sons of the Most High, because he is kind to the ungrateful and wicked.

Be merciful, just as your Father is merciful.

"Do not judge, and you will not be judged. Do not condemn, and you will not be condemned. Forgive, and you will be forgiven.

Luke 6:35-37

THE **A**THLETE'S **T**OPICAL **B**IBLE

But seek first his kingdom and his righteousness, and all these things will be given to you as well.

Matthew 6:33

Treat the older women as mothers, and younger women as sisters, with absolute purity.

1 Timothy 5:2

Blessed are the pure in heart, for they will see God.

Matthew 5:8

Now that you have purified yourselves by obeying the truth so that you have sincere love for your brothers, love one another deeply, from the heart.

1 Peter 1:22

Since we have these promises, dear friends, let us purify ourselves from everything that contaminates body and spirit, perfecting holiness out of reverence for God.

2 Corinthians 7:1

Be devoted to one another in brotherly love. Honor one another above yourselves.

Romans 12:10

It is God's will that you should be sanctified: that you should avoid sexual immorality; that each of you should learn to control his own body in a way that is holy and honorable, not in passionate lust like the heathen, who do not know God.

1 Thessalonians 4:3-5

Live such good lives among the pagans that, though they accuse you of doing wrong, they may see your good deeds and glorify God on the day he visits us.

1 Peter 2:12

Let us behave decently, as in the daytime, not in orgies and drunkenness, not in sexual immorality and debauchery, not in dissension and jealousy.

Romans 13:13

Do not be yoked together with unbelievers. For what do righteousness and wickedness have in common? Or what fellowship can light have with darkness?

What harmony is there between Christ and Belial? What does a believer have in common with an unbeliever?

What agreement is there between the temple of God and idols? For we are the temple of the living God. As God has said: "I will live with them and walk among them, and I will be their God, and they will be my people."

"Therefore come out from them and be separate, says the Lord. Touch no unclean thing, and I will receive you."

"I will be a Father to you, and you will be my sons and daughters, says the Lord Almighty."

2 Corinthians 6:14-18

Flee the evil desires of youth, and pursue righteousness, faith, love and peace, along with those who call on the Lord out of a pure heart.

2 Timothy 2:22

I have written you in my letter not to associate with sexually immoral people.

1 Corinthians 5:9

But my righteous one will live by faith. And if he shrinks back, I will not be pleased with him."

But we are not of those who shrink back and are destroyed, but of those who believe and are saved.

Hebrews 10:38,39

But what does it say? "The word is near you; it is in your mouth and in your heart," that is, the word of faith we are proclaiming.

Romans 10:8

Consequently, faith comes from hearing the message, and the message is heard through the word of Christ.

Romans 10:17

Those who trust in the LORD are like Mount Zion, which cannot be shaken but endures forever.

Psalm 125:1

And we also thank God continually because, when you received the word of God, which you heard from us, you accepted it not as the word of men, but as it actually is, the word of God, which is at work in you who believe.

1 Thessalonians 2:13

David also said to Solomon his son, "Be strong and courageous, and do the work. Do not be afraid or discouraged, for the LORD God, my God, is with you. He will not fail you or forsake you until all the work for the service of the temple of the LORD is finished.

1 Chronicles 28:20

THE ATHLETE'S TOPICAL BIBLE

78

The LORD himself goes before you and will be with you; he will never leave you nor forsake you. Do not be afraid; do not be discouraged."

Deuteronomy 31:8

Early in the morning they left for the Desert of Tekoa. As they set out, Jehoshaphat stood and said, "Listen to me, Judah and people of Jerusalem! Have faith in the LORD your God and you will be upheld; have faith in his prophets and you will be successful."

2 Chronicles 20:20

For it is by grace you have been saved, through faith --and this not from yourselves, it is the gift of God--not by works, so that no one can boast.

Ephesians 2:8,9

But these are written that you may believe that Jesus is the Christ, the Son of God, and that by believing you may have life in his name.

John 20:31

The apostles said to the Lord, "Increase our faith!"

Luke 17:5

We ought always to thank God for you, brothers, and rightly so, because your faith is growing more and more, and the love every one of you has for each other is increasing.

2 Thessalonians 1:3

But you, dear friends, build yourselves up in your most holy faith and pray in the Holy Spirit.

Jude 20

79

The Athlete's Topical Bible

Love is patient, love is kind. It does not envy, it does not boast, it is not proud.

It is not rude, it is not self-seeking, it is not easily angered, it keeps no record of wrongs.

1 Corinthians 13:4,5

Be patient, then, brothers, until the Lord's coming. See how the farmer waits for the land to yield its valuable crop and how patient he is for the autumn and spring rains.

You too, be patient and stand firm, because the Lord's coming is near.

James 5:7,8

Be still before the LORD and wait patiently for him; do not fret when men succeed in their ways, when they carry out their wicked schemes.

Refrain from anger and turn from wrath; do not fret --it leads only to evil.

For evil men will be cut off, but those who hope in the LORD will inherit the land.

Psalm 37:7-9

The end of a matter is better than its beginning, and patience is better than pride.

Do not be quickly provoked in your spirit, for anger resides in the lap of fools.

Ecclesiastes 7:8,9

Be still before the LORD and wait patiently for him; do not fret when men succeed in their ways, when they carry out their wicked schemes.

Psalm 37:7

A man's wisdom gives him patience; it is to his glory to overlook an offense.

Proverbs 19:11

And we urge you, brothers, warn those who are idle, encourage the timid, help the weak, be patient with everyone.

Make sure that nobody pays back wrong for wrong, but always try to be kind to each other and to everyone else.

1 Thessalonians 5:14,15

You too, be patient and stand firm, because the Lord's coming is near.

Don't grumble against each other, brothers, or you will be judged. The Judge is standing at the door!

James 5:8,9

I am not saying this because I am in need, for I have learned to be content whatever the circumstances.

Philippians 4:11

Not only so, but we also rejoice in our sufferings, because we know that suffering produces perseverance; perseverance, character; and character, hope.

And hope does not disappoint us, because God has poured out his love into our hearts by the Holy Spirit, whom he has given us.

Romans 5:3-5

Therefore, as God's chosen people, holy and dearly loved, clothe yourselves with compassion, kindness, humility, gentleness and patience.

Colossians 3:12

But the Lord stood at my side and gave me strength, so that through me the message might be fully proclaimed and all the Gentiles might hear it. And I was delivered from the lion's mouth.

2 Timothy 4:17

He gives strength to the weary and increases the power of the weak.

Isaiah 40:29

The LORD is my strength and my song; he has become my salvation. He is my God, and I will praise him, my father's God, and I will exalt him.

Exodus 15:2

But he said to me, "My grace is sufficient for you, for my power is made perfect in weakness." Therefore I will boast all the more gladly about my weaknesses, so that Christ's power may rest on me.

2 Corinthians 12:9

The LORD is my strength and my song; he has become my salvation.

Psalm 118:14

Surely God is my salvation; I will trust and not be afraid. The LORD, the LORD, is my strength and my song; he has become my salvation."

Isaiah 12:2

Finally, be strong in the Lord and in his mighty power.

Ephesians 6:10

THE ATHLETE'S TOPICAL BIBLE

You armed me with strength for battle; you made my adversaries bow at my feet.

Psalm 18:39

The LORD gives strength to his people; the LORD blesses his people with peace.

Psalm 29:11

A wise man has great power, and a man of knowledge increases strength.

Proverbs 24:5

You armed me with strength for battle; you made my adversaries bow at my feet.

2 Samuel 22:40

I can do everything through him who gives me strength.

Philippians 4:13

The LORD is my strength and my shield; my heart trusts in him, and I am helped. My heart leaps for joy and I will give thanks to him in song.

Psalm 28:7

The LORD is the strength of his people, a fortress of salvation for his anointed one.

Psalm 28:8

But I will sing of your strength, in the morning I will sing of your love; for you are my fortress, my refuge in times of trouble.

Psalm 59:16

The Athlete's Topical Bible

O God, you are my God, earnestly I seek you; my soul thirsts for you, my body longs for you, in a dry and weary land where there is no water.

I have seen you in the sanctuary and beheld your power and your glory.

Psalm 63:1,2

As the deer pants for streams of water, so my soul pants for you, O God.

My soul thirsts for God, for the living God. When can I go and meet with God?

Psalm 42:1,2

Blessed are those who hunger and thirst for righteousness, for they will be filled.

Matthew 5:6

You will seek me and find me when you seek me with all your heart.

Jeremiah 29:13

The LORD is good to those whose hope is in him, to the one who seeks him.

Lamentations 3:25

Come near to God and he will come near to you. Wash your hands, you sinners, and purify your hearts, you double-minded.

James 4:8

The LORD is near to all who call on him, to all who call on him in truth.

Psalm 145:18

84

But if from there you seek the LORD your God, you will find him if you look for him with all your heart and with all your soul.

Deuteronomy 4:29

One thing I ask of the LORD, this is what I seek: that I may dwell in the house of the LORD all the days of my life, to gaze upon the beauty of the LORD and to seek him in his temple.

For in the day of trouble he will keep me safe in his dwelling; he will hide me in the shelter of his tabernacle and set me high upon a rock.

Then my head will be exalted above the enemies who surround me; at his tabernacle will I sacrifice with shouts of joy; I will sing and make music to the LORD.

Hear my voice when I call, O LORD; be merciful to me and answer me.

My heart says of you, "Seek his face!" Your face, LORD, I will seek.

Psalm 27:4-8

But when you pray, go into your room, close the door and pray to your Father, who is unseen. Then your Father, who sees what is done in secret, will reward you.

Matthew 6:6

On my bed I remember you; I think of you through the watches of the night.

Because you are my help, I sing in the shadow of your wings.

My soul clings to you; your right hand upholds me.

Psalm 63:6-8

85

Submit yourselves, then, to God. Resist the devil, and he will flee from you.

Come near to God and he will come near to you. Wash your hands, you sinners, and purify your hearts, you double-minded.

James 4:7,8

I have hidden your word in my heart that I might not sin against you.

Psalm 119:11

Do your best to present yourself to God as one approved, a workman who does not need to be ashamed and who correctly handles the word of truth.

2 Timothy 2:15

Rather, clothe yourselves with the Lord Jesus Christ, and do not think about how to gratify the desires of the sinful nature.

Romans 13:14

In the same way, count yourselves dead to sin but alive to God in Christ Jesus.

Therefore do not let sin reign in your mortal body so that you obey its evil desires.

Do not offer the parts of your body to sin, as instruments of wickedness, but rather offer yourselves to God, as those who have been brought from death to life; and offer the parts of your body to him as instruments of righteousness.

For sin shall not be your master, because you are not under law, but under grace.

Romans 6:11-14

THE ATHLETE'S TOPICAL BIBLE

No, in all these things we are more than conquerors through him who loved us.

Romans 8:37

Then he said to them all: "If anyone would come after me, he must deny himself and take up his cross daily and follow me.

Luke 9:23

The heart is deceitful above all things and beyond cure. Who can understand it?

"I the LORD search the heart and examine the mind, to reward a man according to his conduct, according to what his deeds deserve."

Jeremiah 17:9,10

I have been crucified with Christ and I no longer live, but Christ lives in me. The life I live in the body, I live by faith in the Son of God, who loved me and gave himself for me.

Galatians 2:20

For we know that our old self was crucified with him so that the body of sin might be done away with, that we should no longer be slaves to sin.

Romans 6:6

So I say, live by the Spirit, and you will not gratify the desires of the sinful nature.

Galatians 5:16

Those who belong to Christ Jesus have crucified the sinful nature with its passions and desires.

Galatians 5:24

The integrity of the upright guides them, but the unfaithful are destroyed by their duplicity.

Proverbs 11:3

A perverse man stirs up dissension, and a gossip separates close friends.

Proverbs 16:28

The words of a gossip are like choice morsels; they go down to a man's inmost parts.

Proverbs 18:8

A gossip betrays a confidence; so avoid a man who talks too much.

Proverbs 20:19

For I am afraid that when I come I may not find you as I want you to be, and you may not find me as you want me to be. I fear that there may be quarreling, jealousy, outbursts of anger, factions, slander, gossip, arrogance and disorder.

2 Corinthians 12:20

Without wood a fire goes out; without gossip a quarrel dies down.

Proverbs 26:20

The words of a gossip are like choice morsels; they go down to a man's inmost parts.

Proverbs 26:22

If any of you lacks wisdom, he should ask God, who gives generously to all without finding fault, and it will be given to him.

But when he asks, he must believe and not doubt, because he who doubts is like a wave of the sea, blown and tossed by the wind.

That man should not think he will receive anything from the Lord; he is a double-minded man, unstable in all he does.

James 1:5-8

For the LORD gives wisdom, and from his mouth come knowledge and understanding.

He holds victory in store for the upright, he is a shield to those whose walk is blameless.

Proverbs 2:6,7

The fear of the LORD is the beginning of wisdom; all who follow his precepts have good understanding. To him belongs eternal praise.

Psalm 111:10

Get wisdom, get understanding; do not forget my words or swerve from them.

Proverbs 4:5

When pride comes, then comes disgrace, but with humility comes wisdom.

Proverbs 11:2

And Jesus grew in wisdom and stature, and in favor with God and men.

Luke 2:52

The Athlete's Topical Bible

But now I am writing you that you must not associate with anyone who calls himself a brother but is sexually immoral or greedy, an idolater or a slanderer, a drunkard or a swindler. With such a man do not even eat.

1 Corinthians 5:11

▼ ▼

Do not get drunk on wine, which leads to debauchery. Instead, be filled with the Spirit.

Ephesians 5:18

▼ ▼

Be careful not to make a treaty with those who live in the land where you are going, or they will be a snare among you.

Exodus 34:12

▼ ▼

Wine is a mocker and beer a brawler; whoever is led astray by them is not wise.

Proverbs 20:1

▼ ▼

Woe to those who rise early in the morning to run after their drinks, who stay up late at night till they are inflamed with wine.

Isaiah 5:11

▼ ▼

For you have spent enough time in the past doing what pagans choose to do --living in debauchery, lust, drunkenness, orgies, carousing and detestable idolatry.

They think it strange that you do not plunge with them into the same flood of dissipation, and they heap abuse on you.

But they will have to give account to him who is ready to judge the living and the dead.

1 Peter 4:3-5

▼ ▼

As for you, you were dead in your transgressions and sins, in which you used to live when you followed the ways of this world and of the ruler of the kingdom of the air, the spirit who is now at work in those who are disobedient.

All of us also lived among them at one time, gratifying the cravings of our sinful nature and following its desires and thoughts. Like the rest, we were by nature objects of wrath.

Ephesians 2:1-3

The night is nearly over; the day is almost here. So let us put aside the deeds of darkness and put on the armor of light.

Let us behave decently, as in the daytime, not in orgies and drunkenness, not in sexual immorality and debauchery, not in dissension and jealousy.

Rather, clothe yourselves with the Lord Jesus Christ, and do not think about how to gratify the desires of the sinful nature.

Romans 13:12-14

Listen, my son, and be wise, and keep your heart on the right path.

Do not join those who drink too much wine or gorge themselves on meat.

Proverbs 23:19,20

Do you not know that the wicked will not inherit the kingdom of God? Do not be deceived: Neither the sexually immoral nor idolaters nor adulterers nor male prostitutes nor homosexual offenders nor thieves nor the greedy nor drunkards nor slanderers nor swindlers will inherit the kingdom of God.

1 Corinthians 6:9,10

THE ATHLETE'S TOPICAL BIBLE

Do not be anxious about anything, but in everything, by prayer and petition, with thanksgiving, present your requests to God.

And the peace of God, which transcends all understanding, will guard your hearts and your minds in Christ Jesus.

Philippians 4:6,7

Who of you by worrying can add a single hour to his life?

Since you cannot do this very little thing, why do you worry about the rest?

Luke 12:25,26

Cast all your anxiety on him because he cares for you.

1 Peter 5:7

Trust in the LORD with all your heart and lean not on your own understanding; in all your ways acknowledge him, and he will make your paths straight.

Proverbs 3:5,6

"Come to me, all you who are weary and burdened, and I will give you rest.

Take my yoke upon you and learn from me, for I am gentle and humble in heart, and you will find rest for your souls.

For my yoke is easy and my burden is light."

Matthew 11:28-30

In the day of my trouble I will call to you, for you will answer me.

Psalm 86:7

So do not worry, saying, `What shall we eat?' or `What shall we drink?' or `What shall we wear?'

For the pagans run after all these things, and your heavenly Father knows that you need them.

Matthew 6:31,32

And call upon me in the day of trouble; I will deliver you, and you will honor me."

Psalm 50:15

Cast your cares on the LORD and he will sustain you; he will never let the righteous fall.

Psalm 55:22

For I am the LORD, your God, who takes hold of your right hand and says to you, Do not fear; I will help you.

Isaiah 41:13

"I have told you these things, so that in me you may have peace. In this world you will have trouble. But take heart! I have overcome the world."

John 16:33

Peace I leave with you; my peace I give you. I do not give to you as the world gives. Do not let your hearts be troubled and do not be afraid.

John 14:27

When anxiety was great within me, your consolation brought joy to my soul.

Psalm 94:19

THE ATHLETE'S TOPICAL BIBLE

Rejoice in the Lord always. I will say it again: Rejoice!

Philippians 4:4

▼ ▼

I have told you this so that my joy may be in you and that your joy may be complete.

John 15:11

▼ ▼

For the kingdom of God is not a matter of eating and drinking, but of righteousness, peace and joy in the Holy Spirit.

Romans 14:17

▼ ▼

You have made known to me the path of life; you will fill me with joy in your presence, with eternal pleasures at your right hand.

Psalm 16:11

▼ ▼

The LORD is my strength and my shield; my heart trusts in him, and I am helped. My heart leaps for joy and I will give thanks to him in song.

Psalm 28:7

▼ ▼

For you were once darkness, but now you are light in the Lord. Live as children of light.

Ephesians 5:8

▼ ▼

Though you have not seen him, you love him; and even though you do not see him now, you believe in him and are filled with an inexpressible and glorious joy.

1 Peter 1:8

▼ ▼

Then my soul will rejoice in the LORD and delight in his salvation.

Psalm 35:9

Will you not revive us again, that your people may rejoice in you?

Psalm 85:6

Blessed are those who have learned to acclaim you, who walk in the light of your presence, O LORD.

They rejoice in your name all day long; they exult in your righteousness.

Psalm 89:15,16

Shout for joy to the LORD, all the earth.

Worship the LORD with gladness; come before him with joyful songs.

Psalm 100:1,2

When your words came, I ate them; they were my joy and my heart's delight, for I bear your name, O LORD God Almighty.

Jeremiah 15:16

THE **A**THLETE'S **T**OPICAL **B**IBLE

Each man should give what he has decided in his heart to give, not reluctantly or under compulsion, for God loves a cheerful giver.

2 Corinthians 9:7

The earth is the LORD's, and everything in it, the world, and all who live in it.

Psalm 24:1

For the love of money is a root of all kinds of evil. Some people, eager for money, have wandered from the faith and pierced themselves with many griefs.

1 Timothy 6:10

Keep your lives free from the love of money and be content with what you have, because God has said, "Never will I leave you; never will I forsake you."

Hebrews 13:5

For, "The earth is the Lord's, and everything in it."

1 Corinthians 10:26

The blessing of the LORD brings wealth, and he adds no trouble to it.

Proverbs 10:22

Besides, in my devotion to the temple of my God I now give my personal treasures of gold and silver for the temple of my God, over and above everything I have provided for this holy temple:

1 Chronicles 29:3

But Zacchaeus stood up and said to the Lord, "Look, Lord! Here and now I give half of my possessions to the poor, and if I have cheated anybody out of anything, I will pay back four times the amount."

Jesus said to him, "Today salvation has come to this house, because this man, too, is a son of Abraham.

Luke 19:8,9

And now, brothers, we want you to know about the grace that God has given the Macedonian churches.

Out of the most severe trial, their overflowing joy and their extreme poverty welled up in rich generosity.

For I testify that they gave as much as they were able, and even beyond their ability. Entirely on their own, they urgently pleaded with us for the privilege of sharing in this service to the saints.

2 Corinthians 8:1-4

Command them to do good, to be rich in good deeds, and to be generous and willing to share.

1 Timothy 6:18

"Do not store up for yourselves treasures on earth, where moth and rust destroy, and where thieves break in and steal.

But store up for yourselves treasures in heaven, where moth and rust do not destroy, and where thieves do not break in and steal.

For where your treasure is, there your heart will be also.

Matthew 6:19-21

THE ATHLETE'S TOPICAL BIBLE

Jesus said to her, "I am the resurrection and the life. He who believes in me will live, even though he dies; and whoever lives and believes in me will never die. Do you believe this?"

John 11:25,26

▼ ▼ ▼ ▼ ▼ ▼ ▼ ▼ ▼ ▼ ▼ ▼ ▼ ▼ ▼ ▼ ▼ ▼ ▼ ▼

For there is one God and one mediator between God and men, the man Christ Jesus, who gave himself as a ransom for all men --the testimony given in its proper time.

1 Timothy 2:5,6

▼ ▼ ▼ ▼ ▼ ▼ ▼ ▼ ▼ ▼ ▼ ▼ ▼ ▼ ▼ ▼ ▼ ▼ ▼ ▼

"For God so loved the world that he gave his one and only Son, that whoever believes in him shall not perish but have eternal life.

For God did not send his Son into the world to condemn the world, but to save the world through him.

Whoever believes in him is not condemned, but whoever does not believe stands condemned already because he has not believed in the name of God's one and only Son.

John 3:16-18

▼ ▼ ▼ ▼ ▼ ▼ ▼ ▼ ▼ ▼ ▼ ▼ ▼ ▼ ▼ ▼ ▼ ▼ ▼ ▼

In reply Jesus declared, "I tell you the truth, no one can see the kingdom of God unless he is born again. "

John 3:3

▼ ▼ ▼ ▼ ▼ ▼ ▼ ▼ ▼ ▼ ▼ ▼ ▼ ▼ ▼ ▼ ▼ ▼ ▼ ▼

But he continued, "You are from below; I am from above. You are of this world; I am not of this world.

I told you that you would die in your sins; if you do not believe that I am [the one I claim to be], you will indeed die in your sins."

John 8:23.24

▼ ▼ ▼ ▼ ▼ ▼ ▼ ▼ ▼ ▼ ▼ ▼ ▼ ▼ ▼ ▼ ▼ ▼ ▼ ▼

My sheep listen to my voice; I know them, and they follow me.

I give them eternal life, and they shall never perish; no one can snatch them out of my hand.

My Father, who has given them to me, is greater than all; no one can snatch them out of my Father's hand.

I and the Father are one."

John 10:27-30

▼ ▼

For my Father's will is that everyone who looks to the Son and believes in him shall have eternal life, and I will raise him up at the last day."

John 6:40

▼ ▼

The Father loves the Son and has placed everything in his hands.

Whoever believes in the Son has eternal life, but whoever rejects the Son will not see life, for God's wrath remains on him."

John 3:35,36

▼ ▼

For it is by grace you have been saved, through faith --and this not from yourselves, it is the gift of God-- not by works, so that no one can boast.

Ephesians 2:8,9

▼ ▼

That if you confess with your mouth, "Jesus is Lord," and believe in your heart that God raised him from the dead, you will be saved.

For it is with your heart that you believe and are justified, and it is with your mouth that you confess and are saved.

Romans 10:9,10

▼ ▼

THE ATHLETE'S TOPICAL BIBLE

Forgive us our sins, for we also forgive everyone who sins against us. And lead us not into temptation. '"

Luke 11:4

On reaching the place, he said to them, "Pray that you will not fall into temptation."

"Why are you sleeping?" he asked them. "Get up and pray so that you will not fall into temptation."

Luke 22:40,46

Be careful that you do not forget the LORD your God, failing to observe his commands, his laws and his decrees that I am giving you this day.

But remember the LORD your God, for it is he who gives you the ability to produce wealth, and so confirms his covenant, which he swore to your forefathers, as it is today.

Deuteronomy 8:11,18

Unless the LORD had given me help, I would soon have dwelt in the silence of death.

When I said, "My foot is slipping," your love, O LORD, supported me.

Psalm 94:17,18

My son, if sinners entice you, do not give in to them. My son, do not go along with them, do not set foot on their paths.

Proverbs 1:10,15

"Watch and pray so that you will not fall into temptation. The spirit is willing, but the body is weak."

Matthew 26:41

100

He who walks righteously and speaks what is right, who rejects gain from extortion and keeps his hand from accepting bribes, who stops his ears against plots of murder and shuts his eyes against contemplating evil—this is the man who will dwell on the heights, whose refuge will be the mountain fortress. His bread will be supplied, and water will not fail him.

Isaiah 33:15,16

If your hand or your foot causes you to sin cut it off and throw it away. It is better for you to enter life maimed or crippled than to have two hands or two feet and be thrown into eternal fire.

And if your eye causes you to sin, gouge it out and throw it away. It is better for you to enter life with one eye than to have two eyes and be thrown into the fire of hell.

Matthew 18:8,9

Therefore do not let sin reign in your mortal body so that you obey its evil desires.

Do not offer the parts of your body to sin, as instruments of wickedness, but rather offer yourselves to God, as those who have been brought from death to life; and offer the parts of your body to him as instruments of righteousness.

Romans 6:12,13

Do not be overcome by evil, but overcome evil with good.

Romans 12:21

Be on your guard; stand firm in the faith; be men of courage; be strong.

1 Corinthians 16:13

No temptation has seized you except what is common to man. And God is faithful; he will not let you be tempted beyond what you can bear. But when you are tempted, he will also provide a way out so that you can stand up under it.

1 Corinthians 10:13

He who has been stealing must steal no longer, but must work, doing something useful with his own hands, that he may have something to share with those in need.

Ephesians 4:28

When tempted, no one should say, "God is tempting me." For God cannot be tempted by evil, nor does he tempt anyone; but each one is tempted when, by his own evil desire, he is dragged away and enticed.

Then, after desire has conceived, it gives birth to sin; and sin, when it is full-grown, gives birth to death.

Don't be deceived, my dear brothers.

James 1:13-16

Submit yourselves, then, to God. Resist the devil, and he will flee from you.

James 4:7

Be self-controlled and alert. Your enemy the devil prowls around like a roaring lion looking for someone to devour.

Resist him, standing firm in the faith, because you know that your brothers throughout the world are undergoing the same kind of sufferings.

1 Peter 5:8,9

THE ATHLETE'S TOPICAL BIBLE

I write to you, fathers, because you have known him who is from the beginning. I write to you, young men, because you are strong, and the word of God lives in you, and you have overcome the evil one.

1 John 2:14

Do not conform any longer to the pattern of this world, but be transformed by the renewing of your mind. Then you will be able to test and approve what God's will is --his good, pleasing and perfect will.

Romans 12:2

Set your minds on things above, not on earthly things.

Colossians 3:2

In the same way, the Spirit helps us in our weakness. We do not know what we ought to pray for, but the Spirit himself intercedes for us with groans that words cannot express.

Romans 8:26

So I say, live by the Spirit, and you will not gratify the desires of the sinful nature.

Galatians 5:16

For this reason he had to be made like his brothers in every way, in order that he might become a merciful and faithful high priest in service to God, and that he might make atonement for the sins of the people.

Because he himself suffered when he was tempted, he is able to help those who are being tempted.

Hebrews 2:17,18

Rather, clothe yourselves with the Lord Jesus Christ, and do not think about how to gratify the desires of the sinful nature.

Romans 13:14

For we know that our old self was crucified with him so that the body of sin might be done away with, that we should no longer be slaves to sin.

Romans 6:6

Let your gentleness be evident to all. The Lord is near.

Philippians 4:5

Be self-controlled and alert. Your enemy the devil prowls around like a roaring lion looking for someone to devour.

Resist him, standing firm in the faith, because you know that your brothers throughout the world are undergoing the same kind of sufferings.

1 Peter 5:8,9

Better a patient man than a warrior, a man who controls his temper than one who takes a city.

Proverbs 16:32

"Everything is permissible for me "--but not everything is beneficial. "Everything is permissible for me "--but I will not be mastered by anything.

1 Corinthians 6:12

So I say, live by the Spirit, and you will not gratify the desires of the sinful nature.

Galatians 5:16

The Athlete's Topical Bible

I have been crucified with Christ and I no longer live, but Christ lives in me. The life I live in the body, I live by faith in the Son of God, who loved me and gave himself for me.

Galatians 2:20

Those who belong to Christ Jesus have crucified the sinful nature with its passions and desires.

Galatians 5:24

Dear friends, I urge you, as aliens and strangers in the world, to abstain from sinful desires, which war against your soul.

1 Peter 2:11

Everyone who competes in the games goes into strict training. They do it to get a crown that will not last; but we do it to get a crown that will last forever.

Therefore I do not run like a man running aimlessly; I do not fight like a man beating the air.

No, I beat my body and make it my slave so that after I have preached to others, I myself will not be disqualified for the prize.

1 Corinthians 9:25-27

The end of all things is near. Therefore be clear minded and self-controlled so that you can pray.

1 Peter 4:7

For if you live according to the sinful nature, you will die; but if by the Spirit you put to death the misdeeds of the body, you will live.

Romans 8:13

The Athlete's Topical Bible

Praise be to the God and Father of our Lord Jesus Christ, the Father of compassion and the God of all comfort, who comforts us in all our troubles, so that we can comfort those in any trouble with the comfort we ourselves have received from God.

For just as the sufferings of Christ flow over into our lives, so also through Christ our comfort overflows.

2 Corinthians 1:3-5

And I will ask the Father, and he will give you another Counselor to be with you forever--the Spirit of truth. The world cannot accept him, because it neither sees him nor knows him. But you know him, for he lives with you and will be in you.

I will not leave you as orphans; I will come to you.

John 14:16-18

But the Counselor, the Holy Spirit, whom the Father will send in my name, will teach you all things and will remind you of everything I have said to you.

John 14:26

But you, dear friends, build yourselves up in your most holy faith and pray in the Holy Spirit.

Jude 1:20

Your decrees are the theme of my song wherever I lodge.

Psalm 119:54

I remember your ancient laws, O LORD, and I find comfort in them.

Psalm 119:52

106

David was greatly distressed because the men were talking of stoning him; each one was bitter in spirit because of his sons and daughters. But David found strength in the LORD his God.

1 Samuel 30:6

Even though I walk through the valley of the shadow of death, I will fear no evil, for you are with me; your rod and your staff, they comfort me.

Psalm 23:4

For in the day of trouble he will keep me safe in his dwelling; he will hide me in the shelter of his tabernacle and set me high upon a rock.

Then my head will be exalted above the enemies who surround me; at his tabernacle will I sacrifice with shouts of joy; I will sing and make music to the LORD.

Psalm 27:5,6

I will be glad and rejoice in your love, for you saw my affliction and knew the anguish of my soul.

Psalm 31:7

Cast your cares on the LORD and he will sustain you; he will never let the righteous fall.

Psalm 55:22

My comfort in my suffering is this: Your promise preserves my life.

Psalm 119:50

Blessed are those who mourn, for they will be comforted.

Matthew 5:4

THE ATHLETE'S TOPICAL BIBLE

For the LORD gives wisdom, and from his mouth come knowledge and understanding.

Proverbs 2:6

The works of his hands are faithful and just; all his precepts are trustworthy.

Psalm 111:7

Your statutes stand firm; holiness adorns your house for endless days, O LORD.

Psalm 93:5

The lamp of the LORD searches the spirit of a man; it searches out his inmost being.

Proverbs 20:27

You are my lamp, O LORD; the LORD turns my darkness into light.

2 Samuel 22:29

Lead me, O LORD, in your righteousness because of my enemies-- make straight your way before me.

Psalm 5:8

He guides the humble in what is right and teaches them his way.

Psalm 25:9

Trust in the LORD with all your heart and lean not on your own understanding; in all your ways acknowledge him, and he will make your paths straight.

Proverbs 3:5,6

I will instruct you and teach you in the way you should go; I will counsel you and watch over you.

Psalm 32:8

I desire to do your will, O my God; your law is within my heart."

Psalm 40:8

So I strive always to keep my conscience clear before God and man.

Acts 24:16

Blessed is the man who does not walk in the counsel of the wicked or stand in the way of sinners or sit in the seat of mockers.

But his delight is in the law of the LORD, and on his law he meditates day and night.

He is like a tree planted by streams of water, which yields its fruit in season and whose leaf does not wither. Whatever he does prospers.

Psalm 1:1-3

Whether you turn to the right or to the left, your ears will hear a voice behind you, saying, "This is the way; walk in it."

Isaiah 30:21

If any of you lacks wisdom, he should ask God, who gives generously to all without finding fault, and it will be given to him.

James 1:5

Do two walk together unless they have agreed to do so?

Amos 3:3

You adulterous people, don't you know that friendship with the world is hatred toward God? Anyone who chooses to be a friend of the world becomes an enemy of God.

James 4:4

He who walks with the wise grows wise, but a companion of fools suffers harm.

Proverbs 13:20

He who keeps the law is a discerning son, but a companion of gluttons disgraces his father.

Proverbs 28:7

Stay away from a foolish man, for you will not find knowledge on his lips.

Proverbs 14:7

Do not make friends with a hot-tempered man, do not associate with one easily angered, or you may learn his ways and get yourself ensnared.

Proverbs 22:24,25

A friend loves at all times, and a brother is born for adversity.

Proverbs 17:17

A man of many companions may come to ruin, but there is a friend who sticks closer than a brother.

Proverbs 18:24

Flee the evil desires of youth, and pursue righteousness, faith, love and peace, along with those who call on the Lord out of a pure heart.

2 Timothy 2:22

Blessed is the man who does not walk in the counsel of the wicked or stand in the way of sinners or sit in the seat of mockers.

But his delight is in the law of the LORD, and on his law he meditates day and night.

He is like a tree planted by streams of water, which yields its fruit in season and whose leaf does not wither. Whatever he does prospers.

Psalm 1:1-3

I am a friend to all who fear you, to all who follow your precepts.

Psalm 119:63

Thus you will walk in the ways of good men and keep to the paths of the righteous.

Proverbs 2:20

With whom I once enjoyed sweet fellowship as we walked with the throng at the house of God.

Psalm 55:14

Wounds from a friend can be trusted, but an enemy multiplies kisses.

Proverbs 27:6

As iron sharpens iron, so one man sharpens another.

Proverbs 27:17

THE ATHLETE'S TOPICAL BIBLE

For the wages of sin is death, but the gift of God is eternal life in Christ Jesus our Lord.

Romans 6:23

Even though I walk through the valley of the shadow of death, I will fear no evil, for you are with me; your rod and your staff, they comfort me.

Psalm 23:4

"Do not let your hearts be troubled. Trust in God; trust also in me.

In my Father's house are many rooms; if it were not so, I would have told you. I am going there to prepare a place for you.

And if I go and prepare a place for you, I will come back and take you to be with me that you also may be where I am.

John 14:1-3

Jesus said to her, "I am the resurrection and the life. He who believes in me will live, even though he dies.

John 11:25

For to me, to live is Christ and to die is gain.

Philippians 1:21

However, as it is written: "No eye has seen, no ear has heard, no mind has conceived what God has prepared for those who love him" -- but God has revealed it to us by his Spirit. The Spirit searches all things, even the deep things of God.

1 Corinthians 2:9,10

But our citizenship is in heaven. And we eagerly await a Savior from there, the Lord Jesus Christ.

Philippians 3:20

Just as man is destined to die once, and after that to face judgment.

Hebrews 9:27

For we know that since Christ was raised from the dead, he cannot die again; death no longer has mastery over him.

Romans 6:9

I am the Living One; I was dead, and behold I am alive for ever and ever! And I hold the keys of death and Hades.

Revelation 1:18

For the perishable must clothe itself with the imperishable, and the mortal with immortality.

When the perishable has been clothed with the imperishable, and the mortal with immortality, then the saying that is written will come true: "Death has been swallowed up in victory."

"Where, O death, is your victory? Where, O death, is your sting?"

The sting of death is sin, and the power of sin is the law.

But thanks be to God! He gives us the victory through our Lord Jesus Christ.

1 Corinthians 15:53-57

For it is light that makes everything visible. This is why it is said: "Wake up, O sleeper, rise from the dead, and Christ will shine on you."

Ephesians 5:14

THE ATHLETE'S TOPICAL BIBLE

But the eyes of the LORD are on those who fear him, on those whose hope is in his unfailing love.

Psalm 33:18

The righteous cry out, and the LORD hears them; he delivers them from all their troubles.

Psalm 34:17

He heals the brokenhearted and binds up their wounds.

Psalm 147:3

But those who hope in the LORD will renew their strength. They will soar on wings like eagles; they will run and not grow weary, they will walk and not be faint.

Isaiah 40:31

Dear friends, do not be surprised at the painful trial you are suffering, as though something strange were happening to you.

But rejoice that you participate in the sufferings of Christ, so that you may be overjoyed when his glory is revealed.

1 Peter 4:12,13

He gives strength to the weary and increases the power of the weak.

Isaiah 40:29

So do not fear, for I am with you; do not be dismayed, for I am your God. I will strengthen you and help you; I will uphold you with my righteous right hand.

Isaiah 41:10

114

When you pass through the waters, I will be with you; and when you pass through the rivers, they will not sweep over you. When you walk through the fire, you will not be burned; the flames will not set you ablaze.

Isaiah 43:2

For I am convinced that neither death nor life, neither angels nor demons, neither the present nor the future, nor any powers, neither height nor depth, nor anything else in all creation, will be able to separate us from the love of God that is in Christ Jesus our Lord.

Romans 8:38,39

Praise be to the God and Father of our Lord Jesus Christ, the Father of compassion and the God of all comfort, who comforts us in all our troubles, so that we can comfort those in any trouble with the comfort we ourselves have received from God.

2 Corinthians 1:3,4

God is our refuge and strength, an ever-present help in trouble.

Psalm 46:1

He heals the brokenhearted and binds up their wounds.

Psalm 147:3

Though the mountains be shaken and the hills be removed, yet my unfailing love for you will not be shaken nor my covenant of peace be removed," says the LORD, who has compassion on you.

Isaiah 54:10

115

X's AND O's OF THE FAITH

Quarter

THE ATHLETE'S TOPICAL BIBLE

The precepts of the LORD are right, giving joy to the heart. The commands of the LORD are radiant, giving light to the eyes.

Psalm 19:8

All Scripture is God-breathed and is useful for teaching, rebuking, correcting and training in righteousness.

2 Timothy 3:16

I tell you the truth, until heaven and earth disappear, not the smallest letter, not the least stroke of a pen, will by any means disappear from the Law until everything is accomplished.

Matthew 5:18

Jesus answered, "It is written: `Man does not live on bread alone, but on every word that comes from the mouth of God.' "

Matthew 4:4

Do not let this Book of the Law depart from your mouth; meditate on it day and night, so that you may be careful to do everything written in it. Then you will be prosperous and successful.

Joshua 1:8

He replied, "Blessed rather are those who hear the word of God and obey it."

Luke 11:28

Your word is a lamp to my feet and a light for my path.

Psalm 119:105

Take the helmet of salvation and the sword of the Spirit, which is the word of God.

Ephesians 6:17

For the word of God is living and active. Sharper than any double-edged sword, it penetrates even to dividing soul and spirit, joints and marrow; it judges the thoughts and attitudes of the heart.

Hebrews 4:12

"Every word of God is flawless; he is a shield to those who take refuge in him.

Proverbs 30:5

The unfolding of your words gives light; it gives understanding to the simple.

Psalm 119:130

For these commands are a lamp, this teaching is a light, and the corrections of discipline are the way to life.

Proverbs 6:23

The fear of the LORD is the beginning of wisdom; all who follow his precepts have good understanding. To him belongs eternal praise.

Psalm 111:10

Until I come, devote yourself to the public reading of Scripture, to preaching and to teaching.

1 Timothy 4:13

The Athlete's Topical Bible

But you will receive power when the Holy Spirit comes on you; and you will be my witnesses in Jerusalem, and in all Judea and Samaria, and to the ends of the earth."

Acts 1:8

"The Spirit of the Lord is on me, because he has anointed me to preach good news to the poor. He has sent me to proclaim freedom for the prisoners and recovery of sight for the blind, to release the oppressed, to proclaim the year of the Lord's favor."

Luke 4:18,19

My message and my preaching were not with wise and persuasive words, but with a demonstration of the Spirit's power.

1 Corinthians 2:4

"You are the light of the world. A city on a hill cannot be hidden.

Neither do people light a lamp and put it under a bowl. Instead they put it on its stand, and it gives light to everyone in the house.

In the same way, let your light shine before men, that they may see your good deeds and praise your Father in heaven.

Matthew 5:14-16

Do not tremble, do not be afraid. Did I not proclaim this and foretell it long ago? You are my witnesses. Is there any God besides me? No, there is no other Rock; I know not one."

Isaiah 44:8

"You are my witnesses," declares the LORD, "and my servant whom I have chosen, so that you may know and believe me and understand that I am he. Before me no god was formed, nor will there be one after me.

I, even I, am the LORD, and apart from me there is no savior.

I have revealed and saved and proclaimed-- I, and not some foreign god among you. You are my witnesses," declares the LORD, "that I am God.

Isaiah 43:10-12

▼ ▼

Just as they were handed down to us by those who from the first were eyewitnesses and servants of the word.

Luke 1:2

▼ ▼

You killed the author of life, but God raised him from the dead. We are witnesses of this.

By faith in the name of Jesus, this man whom you see and know was made strong. It is Jesus' name and the faith that comes through him that has given this complete healing to him, as you can all see.

Acts 3:15,16

▼ ▼

The God of our fathers raised Jesus from the dead --whom you had killed by hanging him on a tree.

God exalted him to his own right hand as Prince and Savior that he might give repentance and forgiveness of sins to Israel.

We are witnesses of these things, and so is the Holy Spirit, whom God has given to those who obey him."

Acts 5:30-32

▼ ▼

I desire to do your will, O my God; your law is within my heart."

Psalm 40:8

But Samuel replied: "Does the LORD delight in burnt offerings and sacrifices as much as in obeying the voice of the LORD? To obey is better than sacrifice, and to heed is better than the fat of rams.

1 Samuel 15:22

Trust in the LORD and do good; dwell in the land and enjoy safe pasture.

Commit your way to the LORD; trust in him and he will do this.

Psalm 37:3,5

For the LORD God is a sun and shield; the LORD bestows favor and honor; no good thing does he withhold from those whose walk is blameless.

Psalm 84:11

Instead, you ought to say, "If it is the Lord's will, we will live and do this or that."

James 4:15

For this reason, since the day we heard about you, we have not stopped praying for you and asking God to fill you with the knowledge of his will through all spiritual wisdom and understanding.

Colossians 1:9

THE ATHLETE'S TOPICAL BIBLE

Therefore do not be foolish, but understand what the Lord's will is.

Ephesians 5:17

I desire to do your will, O my God; your law is within my heart."

Psalm 40:8

Teach me to do your will, for you are my God; may your good Spirit lead me on level ground.

Psalm 143:10

For whoever does the will of my Father in heaven is my brother and sister and mother."

Matthew 12:50

But as he left, he promised, "I will come back if it is God's will." Then he set sail from Ephesus.

Acts 18:21

For it is God's will that by doing good you should silence the ignorant talk of foolish men.

1 Peter 2:15

I do not want to see you now and make only a passing visit; I hope to spend some time with you, if the Lord permits.

1 Corinthians 16:7

But Christ has indeed been raised from the dead, the firstfruits of those who have fallen asleep.

1 Corinthians 15:20

After the Sabbath, at dawn on the first day of the week, Mary Magdalene and the other Mary went to look at the tomb.

There was a violent earthquake, for an angel of the Lord came down from heaven and, going to the tomb, rolled back the stone and sat on it.

His appearance was like lightning, and his clothes were white as snow.

The guards were so afraid of him that they shook and became like dead men.

The angel said to the women, "Do not be afraid, for I know that you are looking for Jesus, who was crucified.

He is not here; he has risen, just as he said. Come and see the place where he lay.

Then go quickly and tell his disciples: `He has risen from the dead and is going ahead of you into Galilee. There you will see him.' Now I have told you."

Matthew 28:1-7

As they were coming down the mountain, Jesus gave them orders not to tell anyone what they had seen until the Son of Man had risen from the dead.

Because he was teaching his disciples. He said to them, "The Son of Man is going to be betrayed into the hands of men. They will kill him, and after three days he will rise."

Mark 9:9,31

THE ATHLETE'S TOPICAL BIBLE

That he was buried, that he was raised on the third day according to the Scriptures.

1 Corinthians 15:4

He then began to teach them that the Son of Man must suffer many things and be rejected by the elders, chief priests and teachers of the law, and that he must be killed and after three days rise again.

Mark 8:31

"We are going up to Jerusalem," he said, "and the Son of Man will be betrayed to the chief priests and teachers of the law. They will condemn him to death and will hand him over to the Gentiles, who will mock him and spit on him, flog him and kill him. Three days later he will rise."

Mark 10:33,34

Jesus answered them, "Destroy this temple, and I will raise it again in three days."

The Jews replied, "It has taken forty-six years to build this temple, and you are going to raise it in three days?"

But the temple he had spoken of was his body.

John 2:19-21

For we know that since Christ was raised from the dead, he cannot die again; death no longer has mastery over him.

The death he died, he died to sin once for all; but the life he lives, he lives to God.

In the same way, count yourselves dead to sin but alive to God in Christ Jesus.

Romans 6:9-11

125

THE ATHLETE'S TOPICAL BIBLE

Great is our Lord and mighty in power; his understanding has no limit.

Psalm 147:5

I am the LORD your God; consecrate yourselves and be holy, because I am holy. Do not make yourselves unclean by any creature that moves about on the ground.

Leviticus 11:44

Before the mountains were born or you brought forth the earth and the world, from everlasting to everlasting you are God.

Psalm 90:2

"But will God really dwell on earth? The heavens, even the highest heaven, cannot contain you. How much less this temple I have built!

1 Kings 8:27

Now to the King eternal, immortal, invisible, the only God, be honor and glory for ever and ever. Amen.

1 Timothy 1:17

No one has ever seen God, but God the One and Only, who is at the Father's side, has made him known.

John 1:18

"Who among the gods is like you, O LORD? Who is like you-- majestic in holiness, awesome in glory, working wonders?

Exodus 15:11

Where can I go from your Spirit? Where can I flee from your presence?

If I go up to the heavens, you are there; if I make my bed in the depths, you are there.

If I rise on the wings of the dawn, if I settle on the far side of the sea, even there your hand will guide me, your right hand will hold me fast.

Psalm 139:7-10

A voice says, "Cry out." And I said, "What shall I cry?" "All men are like grass, and all their glory is like the flowers of the field.

The grass withers and the flowers fall, because the breath of the LORD blows on them. Surely the people are grass.

Isaiah 40:6,7

"I the LORD do not change. So you, O descendants of Jacob, are not destroyed.

Malachi 3:6

To whom, then, will you compare God? What image will you compare him to?

Isaiah 40:18

The LORD is righteous in all his ways and loving toward all he has made.

Psalm 145:17

Be perfect, therefore, as your heavenly Father is perfect.

Matthew 5:48

God is spirit, and his worshipers must worship in spirit and in truth."

John 4:24

For to us a child is born, to us a son is given, and the government will be on his shoulders. And he will be called Wonderful Counselor, Mighty God, Everlasting Father, Prince of Peace.

Of the increase of his government and peace there will be no end. He will reign on David's throne and over his kingdom, establishing and upholding it with justice and righteousness from that time on and forever. The zeal of the LORD Almighty will accomplish this.

Isaiah 9:6,7

In the beginning was the Word, and the Word was with God, and the Word was God.

John 1:1

"My food," said Jesus, "is to do the will of him who sent me and to finish his work.

John 4:34

"Do not think that I have come to abolish the Law or the Prophets; I have not come to abolish them but to fulfill them.

Matthew 5:17

For the Son of Man came to seek and to save what was lost."

Luke 19:10

Who gave himself for our sins to rescue us from the present evil age, according to the will of our God and Father,

Galatians 1:4

THE ATHLETE'S TOPICAL BIBLE

The thief comes only to steal and kill and destroy; I have come that they may have life, and have it to the full.

I give them eternal life, and they shall never perish; no one can snatch them out of my hand.

John 10:10,28

For even the Son of Man did not come to be served, but to serve, and to give his life as a ransom for many."

Mark 10:45

God presented him as a sacrifice of atonement, through faith in his blood. He did this to demonstrate his justice, because in his forbearance he had left the sins committed beforehand unpunished.

Romans 3:25

All this is from God, who reconciled us to himself through Christ and gave us the ministry of reconciliation:that God was reconciling the world to himself in Christ, not counting men's sins against them. And he has committed to us the message of reconciliation.

2 Corinthians 5:18,19

He was delivered over to death for our sins and was raised to life for our justification.

Romans 4:25

Since the children have flesh and blood, he too shared in their humanity so that by his death he might destroy him who holds the power of death --that is, the devil.

Hebrews 2:14

May the grace of the Lord Jesus Christ, and the love of God, and the fellowship of the Holy Spirit be with you all.

2 Corinthians 13:14

And I will ask the Father, and he will give you another Counselor to be with you forever--the Spirit of truth. The world cannot accept him, because it neither sees him nor knows him. But you know him, for he lives with you and will be in you.

John 14:16,17

But you will receive power when the Holy Spirit comes on you; and you will be my witnesses in Jerusalem, and in all Judea and Samaria, and to the ends of the earth."

Acts 1:8

But I tell you the truth: It is for your good that I am going away. Unless I go away, the Counselor will not come to you; but if I go, I will send him to you.

When he comes, he will convict the world of guilt in regard to sin and righteousness and judgment: in regard to sin, because men do not believe in me; in regard to righteousness, because I am going to the Father, where you can see me no longer; and in regard to judgment, because the prince of this world now stands condemned.

John 16:7-11

For we were all baptized by one Spirit into one body -- whether Jews or Greeks, slave or free --and we were all given the one Spirit to drink.

1 Corinthians 12:13

THE ATHLETE'S TOPICAL BIBLE

Flesh gives birth to flesh, but the Spirit gives birth to spirit.

You should not be surprised at my saying, `You must be born again.'

The wind blows wherever it pleases. You hear its sound, but you cannot tell where it comes from or where it is going. So it is with everyone born of the Spirit."

John 3:6-8

But when he, the Spirit of truth, comes, he will guide you into all truth. He will not speak on his own; he will speak only what he hears, and he will tell you what is yet to come.

He will bring glory to me by taking from what is mine and making it known to you.

John 16:13,14

Do you not know that your body is a temple of the Holy Spirit, who is in you, whom you have received from God? You are not your own; you were bought at a price. Therefore honor God with your body.

1 Corinthians 6:19,20

And you also were included in Christ when you heard the word of truth, the gospel of your salvation. Having believed, you were marked in him with a seal, the promised Holy Spirit.

Ephesians 1:13

Yet to all who received him, to those who believed in his name, he gave the right to become children of God.

John 1:12

"For God so loved the world that he gave his one and only Son, that whoever believes in him shall not perish but have eternal life.

John 3:16

For all have sinned and fall short of the glory of God.

Romans 3:23

He himself bore our sins in his body on the tree, so that we might die to sins and live for righteousness; by his wounds you have been healed.

1 Peter 2:24

For it is by grace you have been saved, through faith --and this not from yourselves, it is the gift of God--not by works, so that no one can boast.

Ephesians 2:8,9

He who has the Son has life; he who does not have the Son of God does not have life.

I write these things to you who believe in the name of the Son of God so that you may know that you have eternal life.

1 John 5:12,13

Repent, then, and turn to God, so that your sins may be wiped out, that times of refreshing may come from the Lord.

Acts 3:19

In the same way, any of you who does not give up everything he has cannot be my disciple.

Luke 14:33

My sheep listen to my voice; I know them, and they follow me.

I give them eternal life, and they shall never perish; no one can snatch them out of my hand.

My Father, who has given them to me, is greater than all; no one can snatch them out of my Father's hand.

John 10:27-29

But God demonstrates his own love for us in this: While we were still sinners, Christ died for us.

Since we have now been justified by his blood, how much more shall we be saved from God's wrath through him!

Romans 5:8,9

For, "Everyone who calls on the name of the Lord will be saved."

Romans 10:13

I am the gate; whoever enters through me will be saved. He will come in and go out, and find pasture.

John 10:9

He said to me: "It is done. I am the Alpha and the Omega, the Beginning and the End. To him who is thirsty I will give to drink without cost from the spring of the water of life.

Revelation 21:6

THE ATHLETE'S TOPICAL BIBLE

But his delight is in the law of the LORD, and on his law he meditates day and night.

Psalm 1:2

On my bed I remember you; I think of you through the watches of the night.

Psalm 63:6

I meditate on your precepts and consider your ways.
I lift up my hands to your commands, which I love, and I meditate on your decrees.
Oh, how I love your law! I meditate on it all day long.

Psalm 119:15,48,97

My eyes stay open through the watches of the night, that I may meditate on your promises.

Psalm 119:148

I will meditate on all your works and consider all your mighty deeds.

Psalm 77:12

One of those days Jesus went out to a mountainside to pray, and spent the night praying to God.
When morning came, he called his disciples to him and chose twelve of them, whom he also designated apostles.

Luke 6:12,13

Very early in the morning, while it was still dark, Jesus got up, left the house and went off to a solitary place, where he prayed.

Mark 1:35

Do not be anxious about anything, but in everything, by prayer and petition, with thanksgiving, present your requests to God.

And the peace of God, which transcends all understanding, will guard your hearts and your minds in Christ Jesus.

Finally, brothers, whatever is true, whatever is noble, whatever is right, whatever is pure, whatever is lovely, whatever is admirable --if anything is excellent or praiseworthy --think about such things.

Whatever you have learned or received or heard from me, or seen in me --put it into practice. And the God of peace will be with you.

Philippians 4:6-9

On my bed I remember you; I think of you through the watches of the night.

Because you are my help, I sing in the shadow of your wings.

Psalm 63:6-7

But his delight is in the law of the LORD, and on his law he meditates day and night.

He is like a tree planted by streams of water, which yields its fruit in season and whose leaf does not wither. Whatever he does prospers.

Psalm 1:2,3

Do not let this Book of the Law depart from your mouth; meditate on it day and night, so that you may be careful to do everything written in it. Then you will be prosperous and successful.

Joshua 1:8

THE ATHLETE'S TOPICAL BIBLE

Let them praise your great and awesome name-- he is holy.

Exalt the LORD our God and worship at his footstool; he is holy.

Psalm 99:3,5

▼▼▼▼▼▼▼▼▼▼▼▼▼▼▼▼▼▼▼▼▼▼▼▼▼

Yet you are enthroned as the Holy One; you are the praise of Israel.

Psalm 22:3

▼▼▼▼▼▼▼▼▼▼▼▼▼▼▼▼▼▼▼▼▼▼▼▼▼

He provided redemption for his people; he ordained his covenant forever-- holy and awesome is his name.

Psalm 111:9

▼▼▼▼▼▼▼▼▼▼▼▼▼▼▼▼▼▼▼▼▼▼▼▼▼

But you are a chosen people, a royal priesthood, a holy nation, a people belonging to God, that you may declare the praises of him who called you out of darkness into his wonderful light.

1 Peter 2:9

▼▼▼▼▼▼▼▼▼▼▼▼▼▼▼▼▼▼▼▼▼▼▼▼▼

"Who among the gods is like you, O LORD? Who is like you-- majestic in holiness, awesome in glory, working wonders?

Exodus 15:11

▼▼▼▼▼▼▼▼▼▼▼▼▼▼▼▼▼▼▼▼▼▼▼▼▼

And they were calling to one another: "Holy, holy, holy is the LORD Almighty; the whole earth is full of his glory."

Isaiah 6:3

▼▼▼▼▼▼▼▼▼▼▼▼▼▼▼▼▼▼▼▼▼▼▼▼▼

But the LORD Almighty will be exalted by his justice, and the holy God will show himself holy by his righteousness.

Isaiah 5:16

▼▼▼▼▼▼▼▼▼▼▼▼▼▼▼▼▼▼▼▼▼▼▼▼▼

Concerning the prophets: My heart is broken within me; all my bones tremble. I am like a drunken man, like a man overcome by wine, because of the LORD and his holy words.

Jeremiah 23:9

The LORD will lay bare his holy arm in the sight of all the nations, and all the ends of the earth will see the salvation of our God.

Isaiah 52:10

"This, then, is how you should pray: "'Our Father in heaven, hallowed be your name.

Matthew 6:9

God reigns over the nations; God is seated on his holy throne.

Psalm 47:8

Therefore, as God's chosen people, holy and dearly loved, clothe yourselves with compassion, kindness, humility, gentleness and patience.

Colossians 3:12

But you are a chosen people, a royal priesthood, a holy nation, a people belonging to God, that you may declare the praises of him who called you out of darkness into his wonderful light.

1 Peter 2:9

For he chose us in him before the creation of the world to be holy and blameless in his sight. In love

Ephesians 1:4

Seek the LORD while he may be found; call on him while he is near.

Isaiah 55:6

Answer me when I call to you, O my righteous God. Give me relief from my distress; be merciful to me and hear my prayer.

Know that the LORD has set apart the godly for himself; the LORD will hear when I call to him.

Psalm 4:1,3

I call on you, O God, for you will answer me; give ear to me and hear my prayer.

Psalm 17:6

I sought the LORD, and he answered me; he delivered me from all my fears.

Psalm 34:4

Let us draw near to God with a sincere heart in full assurance of faith, having our hearts sprinkled to cleanse us from a guilty conscience and having our bodies washed with pure water.

Hebrews 10:22

And pray in the Spirit on all occasions with all kinds of prayers and requests. With this in mind, be alert and always keep on praying for all the saints.

Ephesians 6:18

This is the confidence we have in approaching God: that if we ask anything according to his will, he hears us.

1 John 5:14

THE ATHLETE'S TOPICAL BIBLE

138

Do not be anxious about anything, but in everything, by prayer and petition, with thanksgiving, present your requests to God.

Philippians 4:6

But when he asks, he must believe and not doubt, because he who doubts is like a wave of the sea, blown and tossed by the wind.

James 1:6

You will seek me and find me when you seek me with all your heart.

Jeremiah 29:13

Then Jesus told his disciples a parable to show them that they should always pray and not give up.

Luke 18:1

In my prayers at all times; and I pray that now at last by God's will the way may be opened for me to come to you.

Romans 1:10

I want men everywhere to lift up holy hands in prayer, without anger or disputing.

1 Timothy 2:8

In the day of my trouble I will call to you, for you will answer me.

Psalm 86:7

139

Praise the LORD, O my soul; all my inmost being, praise his holy name.

Psalm 103:1

Let everything that has breath praise the LORD. Praise the LORD.

Psalm 150:6

When you have eaten and are satisfied, praise the LORD your God for the good land he has given you.

Deuteronomy 8:10

Praise the LORD, O my soul. O LORD my God, you are very great; you are clothed with splendor and majesty.

Psalm 104:1

Praise be to the God and Father of our Lord Jesus Christ, who has blessed us in the heavenly realms with every spiritual blessing in Christ.

Ephesians 1:3

Praise be to the God and Father of our Lord Jesus Christ! In his great mercy he has given us new birth into a living hope through the resurrection of Jesus Christ from the dead.

1 Peter 1:3

Sing to the LORD, you saints of his; praise his holy name.

Psalm 30:4

Let everything that has breath praise the LORD. Praise the LORD.

Psalm 150:6

Enter his gates with thanksgiving and his courts with praise; give thanks to him and praise his name.

Psalm 100:4

Praise the LORD. Praise the LORD, O my soul.

Psalm 146:1

O Lord, open my lips, and my mouth will declare your praise.

Psalm 51:15

Let them praise his name with dancing and make music to him with tambourine and harp.

Psalm 149:3

But you are a chosen people, a royal priesthood, a holy nation, a people belonging to God, that you may declare the praises of him who called you out of darkness into his wonderful light.

1 Peter 2:9

I waited patiently for the LORD; he turned to me and heard my cry.

He lifted me out of the slimy pit, out of the mud and mire; he set my feet on a rock and gave me a firm place to stand.

He put a new song in my mouth, a hymn of praise to our God. Many will see and fear and put their trust in the LORD.

Psalm 40:1-3

COACHES

Quarter

Better a patient man than a warrior, a man who controls his temper than one who takes a city.

Proverbs 16:32

A patient man has great understanding, but a quick-tempered man displays folly.

Proverbs 14:29

A gentle answer turns away wrath, but a harsh word stirs up anger.

Proverbs 15:1

A man's wisdom gives him patience; it is to his glory to overlook an offense.

Proverbs 19:11

It is to a man's honor to avoid strife, but every fool is quick to quarrel.

Proverbs 20:3

Bless those who persecute you; bless and do not curse.
If it is possible, as far as it depends on you, live at peace with everyone.

Romans 12:14,18

Do not cause anyone to stumble, whether Jews, Greeks or the church of God.

1 Corinthians 10:32

Peacemakers who sow in peace raise a harvest of righteousness.

James 3:18

THE ATHLETE'S TOPICAL BIBLE

To slander no one, to be peaceable and considerate, and to show true humility toward all men.

Titus 3:2

Make every effort to live in peace with all men and to be holy; without holiness no one will see the Lord.

Hebrews 12:14

And we urge you, brothers, warn those who are idle, encourage the timid, help the weak, be patient with everyone.

1 Thessalonians 5:14

And the Lord's servant must not quarrel; instead, he must be kind to everyone, able to teach, not resentful.

2 Timothy 2:24

Set a guard over my mouth, O LORD; keep watch over the door of my lips.

Psalm 141:3

He who guards his mouth and his tongue keeps himself from calamity.

Proverbs 21:23

Hide me from the conspiracy of the wicked, from that noisy crowd of evildoers.

Psalm 64:2

My dear brothers, take note of this: Everyone should be quick to listen, slow to speak and slow to become angry.

James 1:19

Resentment kills a fool, and envy slays the simple.

Job 5:2

My lips will not speak wickedness, and my tongue will utter no deceit.

Job 27:4

Set a guard over my mouth, O LORD; keep watch over the door of my lips.

Psalm 141:3

Therefore we do not lose heart. Though outwardly we are wasting away, yet inwardly we are being renewed day by day.

2 Corinthians 4:16

When I called, you answered me; you made me bold and stouthearted.

Psalm 138:3

May our Lord Jesus Christ himself and God our Father, who loved us and by his grace gave us eternal encouragement and good hope, encourage your hearts and strengthen you in every good deed and word.

2 Thessalonians 2:16,17

Being confident of this, that he who began a good work in you will carry it on to completion until the day of Christ Jesus.

Philippians 1:6

He heals the brokenhearted and binds up their wounds.

Psalm 147:3

THE ATHLETE'S TOPICAL BIBLE

146

And when you stand praying, if you hold anything against anyone, forgive him, so that your Father in heaven may forgive you your sins. "

Mark 11:25

Do not repay anyone evil for evil. Be careful to do what is right in the eyes of everybody.

Romans 12:17

Be kind and compassionate to one another, forgiving each other, just as in Christ God forgave you.

Ephesians 4:32

And when you stand praying, if you hold anything against anyone, forgive him, so that your Father in heaven may forgive you your sins. "

Mark 11:25

Forgive us our debts, as we also have forgiven our debtors.

Matthew 6:12

The mouth of the righteous is a fountain of life, but violence overwhelms the mouth of the wicked.

When words are many, sin is not absent, but he who holds his tongue is wise.

Proverbs 10:11,19

A fool shows his annoyance at once, but a prudent man overlooks an insult.

Proverbs 12:16

A gentle answer turns away wrath, but a harsh word stirs up anger.

Proverbs 15:1

Do not repay evil with evil or insult with insult, but with blessing, because to this you were called so that you may inherit a blessing.

1 Peter 3:9

Do not repay anyone evil for evil. Be careful to do what is right in the eyes of everybody.

Romans 12:17

Do not answer a fool according to his folly, or you will be like him yourself.

Proverbs 26:4

Do not be deceived: God cannot be mocked. A man reaps what he sows.

Galatians 6:7

Teach me your way, O LORD; lead me in a straight path because of my oppressors.

Wait for the LORD; be strong and take heart and wait for the LORD.

Psalm 27:11,14

So watch yourselves. "If your brother sins, rebuke him, and if he repents, forgive him.

Luke 17:3

Better is open rebuke than hidden love.

Proverbs 27:5

Cast all your anxiety on him because he cares for you.

1 Peter 5:7

The Athlete's Topical Bible

Instruct a wise man and he will be wiser still; teach a righteous man and he will add to his learning.

Proverbs 9:9

Therefore, as God's chosen people, holy and dearly loved, clothe yourselves with compassion, kindness, humility, gentleness and patience.

Bear with each other and forgive whatever grievances you may have against one another. Forgive as the Lord forgave you.

And over all these virtues put on love, which binds them all together in perfect unity.

And whatever you do, whether in word or deed, do it all in the name of the Lord Jesus, giving thanks to God the Father through him.

Colossians 3:12-14,17

Trust in the LORD with all your heart and lean not on your own understanding; in all your ways acknowledge him, and he will make your paths straight.

Proverbs 3:5,6

Even my close friend, whom I trusted, he who shared my bread, has lifted up his heel against me.

But you, O LORD, have mercy on me; raise me up, that I may repay them.

I know that you are pleased with me, for my enemy does not triumph over me.

Psalm 41:9-11

Do not be deceived: God cannot be mocked. A man reaps what he sows.

Galatians 6:7

149

THE ATHLETE'S TOPICAL BIBLE

But as for me, I will always have hope; I will praise you more and more.

Psalm 71:14

There is surely a future hope for you, and your hope will not be cut off.

Proverbs 23:18

So do not fear, for I am with you; do not be dismayed, for I am your God. I will strengthen you and help you; I will uphold you with my righteous right hand.

Isaiah 41:10

But those who hope in the LORD will renew their strength. They will soar on wings like eagles; they will run and not grow weary, they will walk and not be faint.

Isaiah 40:31

Dear friends, do not be surprised at the painful trial you are suffering, as though something strange were happening to you.

But rejoice that you participate in the sufferings of Christ, so that you may be overjoyed when his glory is revealed.

1 Peter 4:12,13

I know what it is to be in need, and I know what it is to have plenty. I have learned the secret of being content in any and every situation, whether well fed or hungry, whether living in plenty or in want.

I can do everything through him who gives me strength.

Philippians 4:12,13

Let us then approach the throne of grace with confidence, so that we may receive mercy and find grace to help us in our time of need.

Hebrews 4:16

When you pass through the waters, I will be with you; and when you pass through the rivers, they will not sweep over you. When you walk through the fire, you will not be burned; the flames will not set you ablaze.

Isaiah 43:2

For I am convinced that neither death nor life, neither angels nor demons, neither the present nor the future, nor any powers, neither height nor depth, nor anything else in all creation, will be able to separate us from the love of God that is in Christ Jesus our Lord.

Romans 8:38,39

Finally, be strong in the Lord and in his mighty power.

Ephesians 6:10

Be strong and courageous. Do not be afraid or terrified because of them, for the LORD your God goes with you; he will never leave you nor forsake you."

Deuteronomy 31:6

For I know the plans I have for you," declares the LORD, "plans to prosper you and not to harm you, plans to give you hope and a future.

Jeremiah 29:11

The Athlete's Topical Bible

So in everything, do to others what you would have them do to you, for this sums up the Law and the Prophets.

Matthew 7:12

And the second is like it: `Love your neighbor as yourself.'

Matthew 22:39

"Then the King will say to those on his right, `Come, you who are blessed by my Father; take your inheritance, the kingdom prepared for you since the creation of the world.

For I was hungry and you gave me something to eat, I was thirsty and you gave me something to drink, I was a stranger and you invited me in,

I needed clothes and you clothed me, I was sick and you looked after me, I was in prison and you came to visit me.'

Matthew 25:34-36

In everything I did, I showed you that by this kind of hard work we must help the weak, remembering the words the Lord Jesus himself said: `It is more blessed to give than to receive.'"

Acts 20:35

Finally, all of you, live in harmony with one another; be sympathetic, love as brothers, be compassionate and humble.

1 Peter 3:8

Carry each other's burdens, and in this way you will fulfill the law of Christ.

Galatians 6:2

By this all men will know that you are my disciples, if you love one another."

John 13:35

Rejoice with those who rejoice; mourn with those who mourn.

Romans 12:15

And the second is like it: `Love your neighbor as yourself.'

Matthew 22:39

We who are strong ought to bear with the failings of the weak and not to please ourselves.

Romans 15:1

If you really keep the royal law found in Scripture, "Love your neighbor as yourself," you are doing right.

James 2:8

Do not withhold good from those who deserve it, when it is in your power to act.

Do not say to your neighbor, "Come back later; I'll give it tomorrow"-- when you now have it with you.

Proverbs 3:27,28

"Therefore I tell you, do not worry about your life, what you will eat or drink; or about your body, what you will wear. Is not life more important than food, and the body more important than clothes?

Therefore do not worry about tomorrow, for tomorrow will worry about itself. Each day has enough trouble of its own.

Matthew 6:25,34

For the LORD your God is a merciful God; he will not abandon or destroy you or forget the covenant with your forefathers, which he confirmed to them by oath.

Deuteronomy 4:31

So do not fear, for I am with you; do not be dismayed, for I am your God. I will strengthen you and help you; I will uphold you with my righteous right hand.

"All who rage against you will surely be ashamed and disgraced; those who oppose you will be as nothing and perish.

Though you search for your enemies, you will not find them. Those who wage war against you will be as nothing at all.

For I am the LORD, your God, who takes hold of your right hand and says to you, Do not fear; I will help you.

Isaiah 41:10-13

Endure hardship with us like a good soldier of Christ Jesus.

2 Timothy 2:3

"Therefore I tell you, do not worry about your life, what you will eat or drink; or about your body, what you will wear. Is not life more important than food, and the body more important than clothes?

Therefore do not worry about tomorrow, for tomorrow will worry about itself. Each day has enough trouble of its own.

Matthew 6:25,34

The Athlete's Topical Bible

154

Finally, be strong in the Lord and in his mighty power.

Ephesians 6:10

I am not saying this because I am in need, for I have learned to be content whatever the circumstances.

I know what it is to be in need, and I know what it is to have plenty. I have learned the secret of being content in any and every situation, whether well fed or hungry, whether living in plenty or in want.

I can do everything through him who gives me strength.

And my God will meet all your needs according to his glorious riches in Christ Jesus.

Philippians 4:11-13,19

Cast all your anxiety on him because he cares for you.

1 Peter 5:7

He heals the brokenhearted and binds up their wounds.

Psalm 147:3

If any of you lacks wisdom, he should ask God, who gives generously to all without finding fault, and it will be given to him.

James 1:5

What, then, shall we say in response to this? If God is for us, who can be against us?

Romans 8:31

Even in darkness light dawns for the upright, for the gracious and compassionate and righteous man.

He will have no fear of bad news; his heart is steadfast, trusting in the LORD.

Psalm 112:4,7

THE ATHLETE'S TOPICAL BIBLE

Cast your cares on the LORD and he will sustain you; he will never let the righteous fall.

Psalm 55:22

When I said, "My foot is slipping," your love, O LORD, supported me.

When anxiety was great within me, your consolation brought joy to my soul.

Psalm 94:18,19

"Be still, and know that I am God; I will be exalted among the nations, I will be exalted in the earth."

Psalm 46:10

I am not saying this because I am in need, for I have learned to be content whatever the circumstances.

I know what it is to be in need, and I know what it is to have plenty. I have learned the secret of being content in any and every situation, whether well fed or hungry, whether living in plenty or in want.

I can do everything through him who gives me strength.

Philippians 4:11-13

Endure hardship with us like a good soldier of Christ Jesus.

2 Timothy 2:3

So do not fear, for I am with you; do not be dismayed, for I am your God. I will strengthen you and help you; I will uphold you with my righteous right hand.

Isaiah 41:10

156

He alone is my rock and my salvation; he is my fortress, I will never be shaken.

Psalm 62:2

Trust in the LORD with all your heart and lean not on your own understanding; in all your ways acknowledge him, and he will make your paths straight.

Proverbs 3:5,6

Surely God is my salvation; I will trust and not be afraid. The LORD, the LORD, is my strength and my song; he has become my salvation."

Isaiah 12:2

Do not be anxious about anything, but in everything, by prayer and petition, with thanksgiving, present your requests to God.

And the peace of God, which transcends all understanding, will guard your hearts and your minds in Christ Jesus.

Philippians 4:6,7

Who of you by worrying can add a single hour to his life?

Since you cannot do this very little thing, why do you worry about the rest?

Luke 12:25,26

So do not worry, saying, `What shall we eat?' or `What shall we drink?' or `What shall we wear?'

For the pagans run after all these things, and your heavenly Father knows that you need them.

Matthew 6:31,32

So watch yourselves. "If your brother sins, rebuke him, and if he repents, forgive him.

Luke 17:3

Better is open rebuke than hidden love.

Proverbs 27:5

Instruct a wise man and he will be wiser still; teach a righteous man and he will add to his learning.

Proverbs 9:9

The rod of correction imparts wisdom, but a child left to himself disgraces his mother.

Proverbs 29:15

Our fathers disciplined us for a little while as they thought best; but God disciplines us for our good, that we may share in his holiness.

Hebrews 12:10

For attaining wisdom and discipline; for understanding words of insight; for acquiring a disciplined and prudent life, doing what is right and just and fair; for giving prudence to the simple, knowledge and discretion to the young.

Proverbs 1:2-4

Preach the Word; be prepared in season and out of season; correct, rebuke and encourage --with great patience and careful instruction.

2 Timothy 4:2

THE ATHLETE'S TOPICAL BIBLE

These, then, are the things you should teach. Encourage and rebuke with all authority. Do not let anyone despise you.

Titus 2:15

Folly is bound up in the heart of a child, but the rod of discipline will drive it far from him.

Proverbs 22:15

Like an earring of gold or an ornament of fine gold is a wise man's rebuke to a listening ear.

Proverbs 25:12

He who spares the rod hates his son, but he who loves him is careful to discipline him.

Proverbs 13:24

So watch yourselves. "If your brother sins, rebuke him, and if he repents, forgive him.

Luke 17:3

Yet do not regard him as an enemy, but warn him as a brother.

2 Thessalonians 3:15

He who heeds discipline shows the way to life, but whoever ignores correction leads others astray.

Proverbs 10:17

He who ignores discipline comes to poverty and shame, but whoever heeds correction is honored.

Proverbs 13:18

Do not be anxious about anything, but in everything, by prayer and petition, with thanksgiving, present your requests to God.

And the peace of God, which transcends all understanding, will guard your hearts and your minds in Christ Jesus.

Philippians 4:6,7

Cast all your anxiety on him because he cares for you.

1 Peter 5:7

Cast your cares on the LORD and he will sustain you; he will never let the righteous fall.

Psalm 55:22

"Come to me, all you who are weary and burdened, and I will give you rest.

Take my yoke upon you and learn from me, for I am gentle and humble in heart, and you will find rest for your souls.

For my yoke is easy and my burden is light."

Matthew 11:28-30

So do not worry, saying, 'What shall we eat?' or 'What shall we drink?' or 'What shall we wear?'

For the pagans run after all these things, and your heavenly Father knows that you need them.

Matthew 6:31,32

And call upon me in the day of trouble; I will deliver you, and you will honor me."

Psalm 50:15

THE ATHLETE'S TOPICAL BIBLE

"I have told you these things, so that in me you may have peace. In this world you will have trouble. But take heart! I have overcome the world."

John 16:33

Peace I leave with you; my peace I give you. I do not give to you as the world gives. Do not let your hearts be troubled and do not be afraid.

John 14:27

Trust in the LORD with all your heart and lean not on your own understanding; in all your ways acknowledge him, and he will make your paths straight.

Proverbs 3:5,6

He said: "Listen, King Jehoshaphat and all who live in Judah and Jerusalem! This is what the LORD says to you: `Do not be afraid or discouraged because of this vast army. For the battle is not yours, but God's.

2 Chronicles 20:15

I love you, O LORD, my strength.
The LORD is my rock, my fortress and my deliverer; my God is my rock, in whom I take refuge. He is my shield and the horn of my salvation, my stronghold.

Psalm 18:1,2

In the morning, O LORD, you hear my voice; in the morning I lay my requests before you and wait in expectation.

Psalm 5:3

THE ATHLETE'S TOPICAL BIBLE

Therefore wisdom and knowledge will be given you. And I will also give you wealth, riches and honor, such as no king who was before you ever had and none after you will have."

2 Chronicles 1:12

Teach me your way, O LORD; lead me in a straight path because of my oppressors.

Psalm 27:11

Better a patient man than a warrior, a man who controls his temper than one who takes a city.

Proverbs 16:32

`If you belonged to the world, it would love you as its own. As it is, you do not belong to the world, but I have chosen you out of the world. That is why the world hates you.

John 15:19

For the LORD gives wisdom, and from his mouth come knowledge and understanding.

Proverbs 2:6

He who guards his mouth and his tongue keeps himself from calamity.

Proverbs 21:23

If anyone considers himself religious and yet does not keep a tight rein on his tongue, he deceives himself and his religion is worthless.

James 1:26

Whoever gives heed to instruction prospers, and blessed is he who trusts in the LORD.

The wise in heart are called discerning, and pleasant words promote instruction.

Understanding is a fountain of life to those who have it, but folly brings punishment to fools.

A wise man's heart guides his mouth, and his lips promote instruction.

Proverbs 16:20-23

Be wise, my son, and bring joy to my heart; then I can answer anyone who treats me with contempt.

Proverbs 27:11

For God did not give us a spirit of timidity, but a spirit of power, of love and of self-discipline.

2 Timothy 1:7

If any of you lacks wisdom, he should ask God, who gives generously to all without finding fault, and it will be given to him.

James 1:5

When words are many, sin is not absent, but he who holds his tongue is wise.

Proverbs 10:19

Likewise the tongue is a small part of the body, but it makes great boasts. Consider what a great forest is set on fire by a small spark.

James 3:5

THE ATHLETE'S TOPICAL BIBLE

Blessed are the peacemakers, for they will be called sons of God.

Matthew 5:9

If it is possible, as far as it depends on you, live at peace with everyone.

Romans 12:18

If any of you lacks wisdom, he should ask God, who gives generously to all without finding fault, and it will be given to him.

James 1:5

But if you harbor bitter envy and selfish ambition in your hearts, do not boast about it or deny the truth.

For where you have envy and selfish ambition, there you find disorder and every evil practice.

But the wisdom that comes from heaven is first of all pure; then peace-loving, considerate, submissive, full of mercy and good fruit, impartial and sincere.

Peacemakers who sow in peace raise a harvest of righteousness.

James 3:14,16-18

Love is patient, love is kind. It does not envy, it does not boast, it is not proud.

1 Corinthians 13:4

A hot-tempered man stirs up dissension, but a patient man calms a quarrel.

Proverbs 15:18

A perverse man stirs up dissension, and a gossip separates close friends.

Proverbs 16:28

Therefore confess your sins to each other and pray for each other so that you may be healed. The prayer of a righteous man is powerful and effective.

James 5:16

A friend loves at all times, and a brother is born for adversity.

Proverbs 17:17

"A new command I give you: Love one another. As I have loved you, so you must love one another."

John 13:34

Hatred stirs up dissension, but love covers over all wrongs.

Proverbs 10:12

For if you forgive men when they sin against you, your heavenly Father will also forgive you.

But if you do not forgive men their sins, your Father will not forgive your sins.

Matthew 6:14,15

Let us therefore make every effort to do what leads to peace and to mutual edification.

Romans 14:19

If any of you lacks wisdom, he should ask God, who gives generously to all without finding fault, and it will be given to him.

James 1:5

Before his downfall a man's heart is proud, but humility comes before honor.

Proverbs 18:12

Humility and the fear of the LORD bring wealth and honor and life.

Proverbs 22:4

He mocks proud mockers but gives grace to the humble.

Proverbs 3:34

Has not my hand made all these things, and so they came into being?" declares the LORD. "This is the one I esteem: he who is humble and contrite in spirit, and trembles at my word.

Isaiah 66:2

At that time the disciples came to Jesus and asked, "Who is the greatest in the kingdom of heaven?"

He called a little child and had him stand among them.

And he said: "I tell you the truth, unless you change and become like little children, you will never enter the kingdom of heaven.

Therefore, whoever humbles himself like this child is the greatest in the kingdom of heaven.

Matthew 18:1-4

"I tell you that this man, rather than the other, went home justified before God. For everyone who exalts himself will be humbled, and he who humbles himself will be exalted."

Luke 18:14

THE ATHLETE'S TOPICAL BIBLE

But he gives us more grace. That is why Scripture says: "God opposes the proud but gives grace to the humble."

James 4:6

He has brought down rulers from their thrones but has lifted up the humble.

Luke 1:52

The fear of the LORD teaches a man wisdom, and humility comes before honor.

Proverbs 15:33

If my people, who are called by my name, will humble themselves and pray and seek my face and turn from their wicked ways, then will I hear from heaven and will forgive their sin and will heal their land.

2 Chronicles 7:14

He guides the humble in what is right and teaches them his way.

Psalm 25:9

When pride comes, then comes disgrace, but with humility comes wisdom.

Proverbs 11:2

For whoever exalts himself will be humbled, and whoever humbles himself will be exalted.

Matthew 23:12

Take my yoke upon you and learn from me, for I am gentle and humble in heart, and you will find rest for your souls.

Matthew 11:29